Wild Rivers Wild Lands

Ken Madsen

*To the wild things—the plants and
animals that cling obstinately to life in
the face of humanity's destruction of
natural ecosystems, and to the people
who defend the remaining patches of
wildness on our earth.*

Wild Rivers Wild Lands

Ken Madsen

LOST MOOSE

THE YUKON PUBLISHERS

Published by Lost Moose, the Yukon Publishers
58 Kluane Crescent, Whitehorse, Yukon Canada Y1A 3G7
phone (403) 668-5076, 668-3441, fax (403) 668-6223, e-mail: lmoose@yknet.yk.ca
web site: http://www.yukonweb.com/business/lost_moose

Canadian Cataloguing in Publication Data
Madsen, Ken, 1950-
   Wild rivers, wild lands

   (Henderson book series; no. 24)
   ISBN 1-896758-01-0
   1. Wild and scenic rivers--Yukon Territory. 2. Wild and scenic rivers--British Columbia, Northern. 3. Wild and scenic rivers--Alaska. 4. Canoes and canoeing--Yukon Territory. 5. Canoes and canoeing--British Columbia. 6. Canoes and canoeing--Alaska. 7. Wilderness areas--Yukon Territory. 8. Wilderness areas--British Columbia, Northern. 9. Wilderness areas--Alaska. I. Title. II. Series.

GV776.15.Y8M348 1996   917.19'1043   C96-910510-X

Design by Mike Rice
Production and maps by K-L Services, Whitehorse
Printed and bound in Canada
Unless otherwise stated, all photographs are by Ken Madsen

Some of the text and photographs have previously appeared in *Beautiful British Columbia, Canadian Geographic, Nature Canada, Paddler, Up Here* and *Kanawa*.

(facing title page) Mountain caribou above the headwaters of the Stikine River

(title page) Herring gull defending its nest in the Peel Canyon

Henderson Book Series No. 24
The Henderson Book Series honours the kind and generous donation of Mrs. Arthur Henderson, who made this series possible. The Canadian Parks and Wilderness Society gratefully acknowledges Mrs. Henderson's support of our efforts to heighten public awareness of parks and wilderness issues in Canada. To join the Society, please send a donation directly to:

Canadian Parks and Wilderness Society
401 Richmond Street West, Suite 380, Toronto, Ontario, Canada M5V 3A8

Lost Moose gratefully acknowledges the receipt of a Canada Council project grant.

Foreword

One of the most terrifying feelings in my life was the weight against my thighs of a canoe, braced broadside to the current and tipped upstream, as it filled with tons of rushing water, then snapped in half and swept over me to be totally destroyed on the rocks below. I was lucky not to have been killed.

On the other hand, what could be more rewarding than glimpsing that "blue through the trees" which signifies water at the end of a long overland portage, then making a super effort to appear relaxed and strong as you heft your canoe down ever so gently, even though you're really dead tired? Or more soothing than waiting around a campfire for the sweet smell of woodsmoke to waft in your direction to brush away the mosquitoes?

Such are the trials and rewards of wild river and wild land travel—ancient experiences that are happily embedded in the brain, bone and muscle of people like Ken Madsen. Yet, these experiences are being systematically stolen from us and from those who will follow. The river I was raised on in northwestern Ontario nourished me; someone returned the favour by contaminating it with mercury.

This book unashamedly documents the highs of knowing something wonderful, against the lows of fearing it is about to be lost. These kinds of intense contradictions have a way of making a person feel angry and out of formation with contemporary society. They can place you solidly on the fringe, as people begin to wonder whether *you* aren't losing it!

But in reality it is civilized society which is out of touch with reality. When asked what he thought of civilization, Ghandi is reported to have responded, "It would be nice."

We are likely the last generation with the opportunity to draw a line in the sand while it will still make a difference, to insist that at least representative samples, if not large wilderness tracts, of our God-given lands and waters remain in a natural state. Yet, as we are put to the test, with a road or a mine here, a dam or a cutblock there, we are increasingly unable to simply leave wild things alone. So wilderness doesn't just passively "disappear." Rather, it is deliberately degraded, chipped away and eliminated by thousands of disassociated decisions which add up to a terrible and permanent loss.

Read Ken's book. Then ask yourself, "Do I want this to become a nice historical record of how things used to be? Or will I do something to determine how things *will* be?"

Monte Hummel
President, World Wildlife Fund Canada

Spruce skeleton beside the Alsek River

Acknowledgements

I would like to thank the following people who helped with the creation of this book—and put up with my idiosyncrasies during river trips:

Wendy Boothroyd: for her patience and editorial skills.

Glen Davis: a generous supporter of the World Wildlife Fund's Endangered Spaces Campaign and volunteer editor of this book.

Derek Endress: paddling partner and member of the Tatshenshini Wilderness Quest.

Monte Hummel: a man who is busy with the many important programs of the World Wildlife Fund, but who still found time to write the eloquent foreward for this book.

Katy Madsen: my mother—her dedication to the environment started me along the path towards work on wilderness preservation.

Kirsten Madsen: a talented writer and editor whose suggestions greatly improved this book.

Polly Madsen: for her encouragement and editorial help.

Juri Peepre: a tireless defender of the natural world and great wilderness companion who helped with the Wildlands section of this book.

Ian Pineau: paddling partner and member of Tatshenshini Wilderness Quest.

Jody Schick: member of the Tatshenshini Wilderness Quest and level-headed paddling partner who helped me safely experience the rivers in this book.

Rachel Shepard: a friend who sat with me in a cold aluminum canoe all the way down the Alsek River and who gave editorial advice.

The following people motivated and inspired me in my environmental work, writing and photography: Malcolm Alsek Boothroyd • Margot Boothroyd • Cindy Breitkreutz • Joe Charlie • Ron Cruikshank • Frank Doyle • Stewart Elgie • Mary Granskou • Willard Hagen • Bob Jickling • Sue Johnson • Matthew Lien • Sarah Locke • Lost Moose Publishing • Sharon MacCoubrey • Joyce Majiski • Paul Mason • Jocylyn McDowell • Jill Pangman • Alex Peepre • Steve Philp • Jack Schick • Joanne Schick • Tony Shaw • George Smith • Charlie Snowshoe • Arno Springer • Kate Williams • George Wuerthner

Contents

Sunset over Wolf Lake

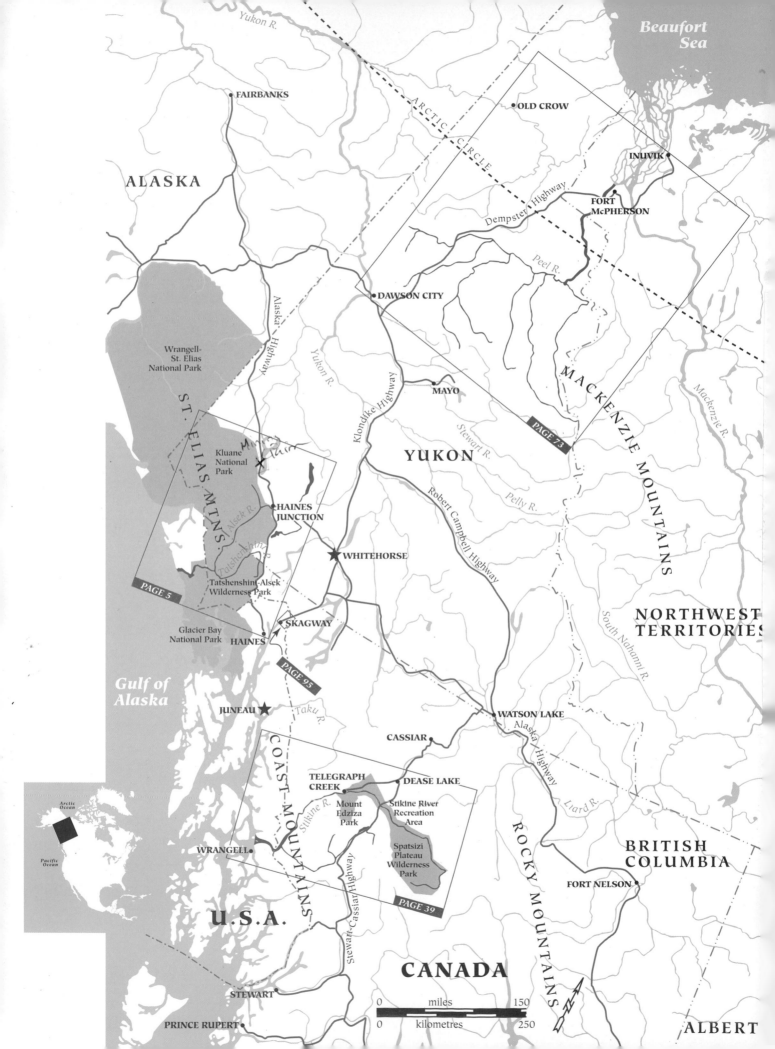

Introduction

"I know the nest is here somewhere," says my daughter Kirsten. "Keep your eyes open. The female might attack if you approach her nest."

I crouch down, imagining needle-sharp talons raking my scalp. Kirsten scrambles over fallen trees, searching for snags where goshawks perch and tear apart their prey: ptarmigan, grouse and squirrels. She is looking for signs: feathers, bones or whitewash.

"There it is." She points towards a tall spruce. I have trouble finding the nest, then I see a pair of fuzzy white fluffballs standing out against a dark tangle of sticks. "The mother isn't in attack mode yet, the chicks are too young for her to be off the nest." Kirsten hands me her binoculars. The goshawk jumps into focus.

She is slate grey, her bold dark head slashed by a pale stripe through the eyes. She is motionless, staring at us with blood-red eyes. An instinct is whispering to her, telling her to launch from the nest like a feathered bolt of lightning. But for the moment, something stronger is holding her tight to her chicks. Voltage arcs from her eyes to mine. The electricity in those eyes is the glowing fire of wildness.

Later in the day I follow Kirsten and Frank Doyle up a broad glacial stream-bed. We're looking for a red-tailed hawk's nest. Frank is a biologist studying raptors at the Arctic Institute, near Kluane Lake in the southern Yukon. Kirsten, who just graduated from university, is working with him for the summer. As we walk, Frank tells me about goshawks, how they defend their nests with single-minded violence.

I think about the beauty of it, the fury of it. A bird smaller than a raven, a couple of pounds of muscle, sinew and feathers, screaming "kak, kak, kak," attacking a full-grown human. Fighting for the survival of its young—for the survival of its species.

"If you looked at a goshawk in Europe, you wouldn't be able to tell it apart from the ones here," says Frank. "Same size, same red eyes, same plumage. But they don't defend their young. When people approach they slip off through the forest, more like a warbler than a goshawk."

Frank hops nimbly over a log and strides into the forest. I trot to keep up. "Why are European goshawks so different?"

"There is a widely-held theory that natural selection created timid goshawks. The rich landowners wanted to save game birds for their hunting parties. They didn't want wild hawks eating grouse. Gamekeepers could easily find the nests of aggressive goshawks and destroy them. Over hundreds of years, the hawks that defended their nests were wiped out. The shy ones were left, the timid ones. It's the same with bears. The European bear is a shy, nocturnal creature."

I stop walking and look around me. The spruce forest is like a warm green blanket on the lower slopes of Kluane's Front Range. Across the valley is Kluane Lake and the Ruby Range. I can almost pretend that these wildlands go on forever. The drone of a truck on the Alaska Highway brings me back to reality.

In much of North America we've slaughtered the wolves and the grizzlies and the mountain lions. We've taken the "wild" from the wilderness. In Europe they've gone a step further—they've even removed the wild from wildlife like goshawks and bears. The north's harsh climate, rugged terrain, and distance from markets have spared it from being a major battlefield in the war between humans and wildness—but it is no longer a safe haven.

The Yukon government is killing wolves near here. Gunning them down from planes, trapping them, snaring them. Like European gentry, the politicians don't want to feed "their" caribou and moose to wild carnivores. Loggers are itching to clear-cut the forest we are walking through. On slopes above Kluane Lake, the scars from mineral exploration slash across alpine meadows. Similar scenes are happening across the Yukon.

Wildness in the natural world is wholeness. Wildness doesn't need to be improved by development. It doesn't require our moral approval or legislative authority. Wildness is. The stories in this book come from watersheds that are as wild as they can be in the midst of our technological world.

Here's to goshawks! I hope we display as much courage when it comes to the ultimate defence of the wild earth.

The Alsek-Tatshenshini Watershed

The Alsek-Tatshenshini Watershed

"I'm going to puke," groaned the small boy in front of me.

"Not again," said his mother, thrusting a plastic bag under his chin. We lurched in the crosswind. My normally reliable stomach heaved doubtfully as the sour odour of second-hand vomit wafted through the plane.

We banked away from the Tatshenshini River and flew over a deep canyon leading towards Geddes Resources' exploration camp near Windy Craggy Mountain. We zipped over a cluster of deserted buildings and a long gravel airstrip. The miners had gone home while politicians were trying to untangle the knot of controversy surrounding the proposed mine near the Tatshenshini.

Windy Craggy has a classic summit, a pyramid that a Toronto-based mining company wanted to blast away. With a shuffle of paper and an infusion of shareholders' money the company planned to flex its corporate muscle and cast the mountain onto the glacier. I could see the exploration shaft drilled into Windy Craggy's flanks. A red streak of acid-rock drainage dribbled from the mountain, like blood seeping from a puncture wound.

We turned away from the mountain and droned over the Tats Glacier. "That's where they plan to put their pipeline," said Bill, the pony-tailed pilot from "Lighthawk," an environmental organization that provides air transport for conservation groups.

"A toxic pipeline on an active glacier is a frightening thought," I remarked.

Our words were directed towards the boy's father, the man sitting in the copilot's seat, the president of a wealthy foundation. My job was to convince him that it was urgent to protect this watershed, to convince him to bring out his chequebook for the cause. I couldn't tell if he was impressed. Maybe he felt like throwing up too.

We swooped over the low pass that separated the Tatshenshini watershed from the Alsek. "They would need foolproof dams at both ends of their tailings lake," I said. "A breach at the south end would flood acid drainage into the Tatshenshini. At this end, acid would spill into the Alsek."

(previous pages) Morning mist beside the Tatshenshini River

Autumn light above the upper Alsek River

"And this is one of the most volatile earthquake zones on earth," said Bill.

We buzzed up the Alsek and over Turnback Canyon. The land looked unimpressive from up here, like a toy wilderness, as if Fisher-Price had set out model valleys and glaciers. The plane's height and speed distorted our perception of the size and power of the land.

The first time I paddled the Alsek River we camped directly below here, beside the Tweedsmuir Glacier. I remembered grizzly tracks on the snow and the scream of an ice-avalanche that sounded like a 747 lifting off beside my sleeping bag. I remembered the storm that tried to flatten our tent. I remembered the St. Elias Mountains looking like clouds above the glacier, and a butterfly on the ice, wings outstretched, soaking up the scant warmth of the late September sun.

I remembered feeling tiny. Insignificant. A good feeling.

"You'll have to come back and do a river trip," I said. "It's only when your feet are on the ground that you can appreciate

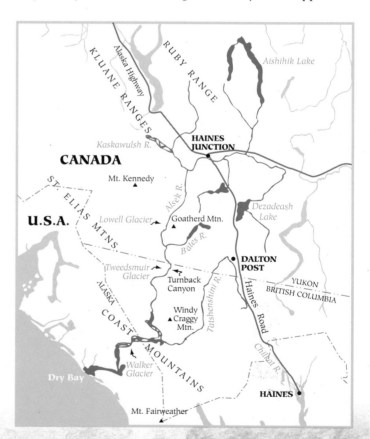

the grandeur of this area." I was trying to speak from the heart, but my words sounded lame, as if I was advertising "$1.49 Day" in the wilderness.

Peering down from the plane reconfirmed one thing: the importance of the low elevation river valleys. At that time, the Alsek and Tatshenshini were surrounded by national parks: Kluane in the Yukon, Glacier Bay and Wrangell-St. Elias in Alaska. Parks of snow and ice with the highest mountains in Canada and the largest non-polar ice fields in the world. Parks created in the usual, deeply flawed North American method—preserve the monumental scenery, let the developers have the productive wildlife habitat.

There are only two green threads in this sea of mountains, the forested slopes beside the Alsek and Tatshenshini. These rivers are spawning grounds for all five species of Pacific salmon. These valleys are the home of mountain goats, Dall sheep, moose, wolves, rare silver-blue glacier bears and an astonishing density of grizzly bears.

"Road access into the Tatshenshini would be the end of the wilderness," I said to the potential donor as we touched down in Whitehorse. We shook hands and he and his family strolled back to their rental car. I was left wondering if I had wasted my time by trying to sell wilderness, playing the money game. Bill was left holding a bag of vomit.

_____ ◊ _____ ◊ _____ ◊

My first taste of advocacy in the Tatshenshini-Alsek wilderness happened in 1986, a protest about a placer gold mine that is a cancerous spot in the Tatshenshini's upper canyon. I sat through endless hearings, but I quickly became bored of playing by the government's rules, rules that ensured we couldn't win.

I staked a mining claim at the historic site of Dalton Post to point out the idiocy of Yukon mining legislation that dates back to 1917. Government bureaucrats were angry that I had the gall to stake a claim when I had no intention of mining. They threatened a fourteen-year jail term for swearing a false affidavit. They eventually disallowed my claim on a technicality.

Kirsten Madsen tenting in the coastal paintbrush beside the Alsek River

Meanwhile, Geddes Resources was quietly working on a much bigger scheme, a proposed open-pit copper mine at Windy Craggy Mountain. Geddes wanted to build an all-weather road through the wilderness, lay down 250 kilometres of pipeline, dig massive tailings lakes and dynamite the top off the mountain.

I jumped into the campaign because I was naive enough to believe that we could win. Idealistic enough to believe that the interests of grizzlies, salmon and bald eagles could compete with the mining-money machine. Pig-headed enough to keep struggling.

For the first few years it was a lonely vigil. I wrote letters to faceless bureaucrats. I talked with the media. I organized slide shows. My audiences were polite. They agreed that the watershed should be preserved. But they asked, "Do you know how much money Geddes Resources has invested?"

About the same time that I started campaigning in the north, groups in British Columbia also began to lobby against the Windy Craggy Project. Alaskans grew concerned about threats to Glacier Bay National Park, their salmon fisheries and to eagles in the Chilkat Bald Eagle Preserve. We joined forces and created Tatshenshini International, a coalition of environmental groups whose membership totalled in the millions. The campaign caught fire.

My main contribution was the "Tatshenshini Wilderness Quest," a "paddle-a-thon" down the three rivers that would have been most affected by the proposed mine: the Chilkat, the Tatshenshini and the Alsek. We collected sponsorships through the World Wildlife Fund to raise money, generated publicity and put together a slide show that I toured across North America.

We were lucky. The threats to wildlands posed by the Windy Craggy project were so obscene that even politicians couldn't ignore them. A flood of letters washed up on the desk of the Premier of British Columbia, Mike Harcourt.

In June, 1993, the British Columbia (B.C.) government created the Tatshenshini-Alsek Wilderness Park. The following year UNESCO (United Nations Educational, Scientific and Cultural Organization) declared it a World Heritage Site. It is the critical component of what is now one of the largest international wilderness reserves on the planet.

The mining community thinks it's an anomaly. An outrage against God and the Gross National Product. I think it's just the beginning.

CAPTAIN HOOK VISITS MT. FAIRWEATHER

The telephone rang one Yukon June evening back in 1985, when the sunshine was ricocheting around the yard and the only place I wanted to be was outside. I walked up the back steps into the kitchen and reluctantly picked up the phone.

"Hello! This is Joanne Schick. My two sons are registered in your rock climbing course."

"Yes?" I hoped my tone sounded more enthusiastic than I felt. At the time I was a teacher. With school nearly out for the summer, I looked forward to another parent-teacher chat like I look forward to a case of tonsillitis.

"Jody is almost twelve, a year younger than your minimum age," she said, "but he's really keen."

Mothers! I thought. The kid probably spends all day in the basement in front of the tube. This is probably a ploy to get him outside before he turns furry and squinty-eyed like a mole.

"Where have you taught climbing before?" Jody's mother asked the question casually, as if safety wasn't a big issue. As if she wouldn't be at my throat if Jody got hurt. If she had known what he and I would be up to in the next few years, she would have chained him in the basement.

Jody survived the climbing course. A couple of weeks later I saw him down at the Yukon River. He was wearing a patched wet suit and paddling an over-sized fibreglass kayak. Modern kayaks are designed to fit your body like lycra tights, but Jody flopped around in his huge boat like a salmon in a skiff.

His mother was right. He *was* keen. He'd flip over, eject from his kayak and swim to shore as if no one had yet invented the Eskimo roll. Then he'd grin and do it again. He improved quickly. He saved his money and bought a smaller kayak. He learned to roll. We started paddling together. Maybe Jody was exceptionally mature for his age. Maybe I was exceptionally immature. We became friends.

People thought it was weird that Jody and I were such good friends. After all, he was younger than my older daughter. I didn't care. Conversations between men are often superficial—cleverly constructed to conceal feelings. When

Jody had something to say, he said it. Our talks were fresh and direct, stripped of any veneer of sophistication.

Jody was never afraid to put his foot in his mouth. He had sailed through elementary school without becoming paranoid about saying things that were "stupid," unlike most kids. Unlike me. I remember grade four. Standing beside the blackboard, blushing in shame while the teacher corrected me and the class giggled. Spending time with Jody brought me back to the days when talking was pure fun. To the days before the things you said had to make sense.

The first long kayak trip that Jody and I did together was the "first descent" of the Bates River. The Bates flows through the southern end of Kluane National Park and spills into the Alsek River. The Alsek watershed is a enchanted place. It's like Neverland, from the classic children's tale, *Peter Pan*. In both places there are no "tedious distances between one adventure and another."

We scheduled two weeks to reach our take-out at Dry Bay, Alaska. Along the way, there was the small matter of Turnback Canyon to deal with.

Jody had become interested in Turnback Canyon years earlier, at an age when most kids are obsessed with Big Bird and the Cookie Monster. Jody grew up in Haines Junction, the gateway to Kluane and the Alsek River. His father worked in Kluane National Park and was also fascinated by the Alsek. Several of the early groups to run the river used the Schick home as a base to sort gear and pack food.

In 1981, an international expedition landed on the Schick doorstep. The group intended to become the first Europeans to paddle Turnback Canyon. Jody, who was then seven, played in the mounds of gear and pestered the kayakers with questions. Thierry Giorgetti, a French paddler and the youngest member of the team, let Jody sit in his kayak and pretend he was paddling Turnback Canyon.

Several days later, Giorgetti drowned in violent rapids at the beginning of the canyon. The expedition was aborted and the kayaks and gear airlifted back to Haines Junction. Several of the boats found their way to the Schick's back yard. Jody later learned to paddle in one of these kayaks, down at the Yukon River.

Jody Schick kayaking on the Tatshenshini River

Joanne Schick thinks that Turnback Canyon is a cross between Niagara Falls and Hades. Before Jody and I left for the Bates River, she pierced me with a laser-beam stare. "You *are* going to portage around Turnback Canyon, aren't you?" Her fingers drummed the kitchen table and her voice rose. "Jody is not to go anywhere near that canyon."

We paddle cautiously down the Bates River, which turns out to be peppered with difficult rapids. After four days we flush through a deep, rusty-orange canyon and float into the Alsek. The water is the colour of quicksand, an infusion of glacial silt that hisses and pops against the hard plastic of our kayaks.

The next day we set up camp above Turnback Canyon. The river is flooded with glacial runoff and the rapids look horrible. The whitewater swirls and boils explosively, as if pirates are firing cannonballs into the river.

The route around Turnback Canyon is across the massive Tweedsmuir Glacier and must be one of the longest portages in the world. It is hot. Heat waves shimmer off the jumbled rock of the terminal moraine and distort our view of the St. Elias Mountains. We jury-rig harnesses to carry our kayaks and struggle across the glacier. We stagger back to the river two strenuous days later, muscles stiff, bodies bruised, boots in tatters.

Paddling again is a delight, even when clouds swarm up from the Pacific and crawl down the mountainsides. The Alsek Valley becomes a grey tunnel. Rain slants into our faces. We paddle past the confluence of the Tatshenshini, past the Walker Glacier, past the international border into Alaska. I smell the ocean in the wind. The salt breeze murmurs that the end of our trip is near.

The dark face of the storm glowers for days. When blue patches of sky finally wink at us, they look too bright to be real. Mist shimmers like gauzy curtains blowing in an open window. Mountains appear above the clouds. One peak is so much bigger than its neighbours it seems to be floating in the sky, as if it is enchanted.

"That's Mt. Fairweather," I shout to Jody, who is drifting lazily nearby. "Almost five thousand metres high, rising straight out of the ocean."

"Why is it called Fairweather?"

The glaciers that flow into the Alsek valley make it obvious that the weather is seldom fair here. Moisture-laden storms sweep in from the Pacific, batter the mountains and dump tons of snow. The snow packs down, compresses and creeps back to the river as glacial ice.

"Captain Cook named it," I yell. An errant current pushes Jody towards shore, so I paddle closer. "It must have been a sunny day when he sailed up the coast and saw Fairweather. It was during his last voyage, just before he was killed by natives in Hawaii."

Jody is quiet as we float along. The clouds reassert their dominance, chasing away the blue. The mountains disappear. The summit of Fairweather is the last to go.

"Captain Cook," says Jody thoughtfully. "Was that the guy in Peter Pan?"

Jody paddling near an ice wall beside Alsek Lake and (right) playing or doing an "ender" on the Tatshenshini River

PADDLING WITH NATIONAL GEOGRAPHIC

The Alsek River laps against the canoe. I pull out a food bag and dump it on shore. It crunches on the gravel next to a heap of tents, sleeping bags, ice axes, camera cases, tripods, ropes and a fire-pan. "We should have a garage sale," says Rachel, lifting out a single-side-band radio that's as heavy as a lump of lead.

We don't normally haul radios into the wilderness, but this trip is part adventure, part publicity stunt. We hope to publicize the Tatshenshini-Alsek issue by calling the CBC radio network from the wilderness. Our attempt to become radio personalities will depend upon atmospheric conditions. If we can reach NorthwesTel, they can theoretically patch us through to CBC in Toronto.

It is mid-September, 1991, and Derek Endress, Ian Pineau, Jody Schick and I are on the last river trip of our "Tatshenshini Wilderness Quest." Since we're hauling tons of gear down the Alsek, my friend Rachel Shephard and I are paddling an ancient aluminum canoe that doubles as a cargo barge. The others are towing my kayak.

Judging by the tracks on the beach, our neighbours at this camp on the Alsek are mainly grizzlies. I'm glad that bears aren't protective of private property, like humans. Property values in the wilderness usually go way down when people arrive.

We carry the canoe up the beach and flip it over. After Rachel and I set up our tent, I decide to explore our new neighbourhood. To get a better view, I clamber up an old volcanic cliff, searching for footholds in the splintered, orange-hued lava.

I squat on a ledge, looking and listening. The valley is full of noise: the moan of the wind, a drip of meltwater, the whoosh-whoosh of a raven's wingbeats, a sharp crack as Derek pounds tent pegs. Across the river, thick clouds writhe in the wind. Fragments of mountains appear and vanish in the mist: here a steely-blue chunk of glacier, there a bit of razor-sharp ridge.

Down at camp, Rachel and Jody are stretched out in a field of fluffy dryas seed-pods. Ian sprawls on a granite

Ian Pineau writes in his journal beside the Alsek River

boulder, writing in his journal. Derek fiddles with the stove. The thought of a hot drink lures me down. Soon I'm cradling a mug of thick, sweet tea, feeling the warmth seep through the plastic into my chilled fingers.

"Let's see if we can reach the NorthwesTel operator," says Derek, pulling the radio out of its dry-bag. He checks the batteries, plugs in jacks and flips knobs. He hands Ian and I each a spool of antenna wire. "Spread it out like a giant letter 'T' on the beach."

Derek hunches over the radio and presses the transmit button on the microphone. "NorthwesTel operator, this is SQ 647. Do you copy? Over." We hear a steady hiss, punctuated by pops and burps. "Change the angle of the antenna," Derek shouts. Ian and I swivel the wire and drape it over a pair of boulders. "That's better, I hear something now."

"I miss you darling. Do you know how much I love you?" It's not the operator. We're listening to a couple of sweethearts talk on their radiophones somewhere in northern B.C.

"Well, it's real cold up here. Ice on the lake this morning. No moose yet."

I picture a man at a hunting camp. He's wearing a denim jacket and rubbing the toe of his cowboy boot in the dirt. He's willing to talk about the weather or hunting, but not about love.

"This is bizarre," says Rachel. "I've never before eavesdropped on a conversation from the wilderness."

"Let's see if we can pick up something on the mining channel," mutters Derek. He flicks the knob to another setting and a startlingly clear voice jumps into camp, "The boys and I are getting tired of stale crackers up here. Can anyone give us a recipe for bread? Over."

"Is that you Verne? This is Betty at Big Creek. Okay. Mix a package of yeast with two cups of warm water...."

"This is like channel surfing," says Ian. "First we get *As the World Turns*, then the *Galloping Gourmet*."

"I'll try one more frequency," says Derek, fiddling with the dials.

Then we hear a scratchy voice. "Alsek Expedition, Alsek Expedition, this is National Geographic. Over!"

"Hey!" says Derek. "Here Ken, you talk to him." He hands me the microphone.

"National Geographic, this is the Alsek Expedition."

13

"He can't hear you," says Derek. "You have to push the transmit button on the microphone."

"Oh." I press the button. "National Geographic, this is the Alsek Expedition."

"Say over," says Derek patiently.

"Over!"

"Alsek Expedition, this is Dirk Freeman, photographer for *National Geographic*. I want to photograph you in Turnback Canyon and I need to book a helicopter. What's your schedule? Over."

"Well, it'll depend on the weather and the water level...."

"Alsek Expedition, you're fading out! Count to ten and I'll monitor your levels. Over."

"What the...?" I look at Derek. He shrugs. I start counting, "One, two, three...nine, ten. Over."

"Okay! Now, when will you paddle the canyon? Over."

"Look, we hope to give it a shot on September 25th, but it depends...."

"Right, Alsek Expedition!" he says briskly "I copy you. You'll be running Turnback Canyon on September two-five. Monitor the radio at 8:00 p.m. on September two-three and we'll reconfirm. Over and out."

"Should we try NorthwesTel again?" asks Derek.

"Just shut the thing off," says Rachel, her tone exasperated, as if someone is forcing her to watch an episode of *Three's Company*.

I slide the microphone back on its hook and flip off the power. The static crackle fades. Only gradually do the sounds of the land creep back: the rustle of alder leaves, the gurgle of the river, the rattle of rocks sliding down an eroded cut bank.

✄   ✄   ✄

We are collecting sponsorships for our Wilderness Quest to raise money for the Tatshenshini campaign. Our main goal though, is the difficult task of generating publicity. Unfortunately, journalists are preoccupied with the financial beat: the Canadian dollar's struggle against the U.S. dollar and its struggle with the yen. The Gross National Product is more riveting than Gross Northern Pollution.

Jody floating near icebergs beneath the St. Elias Mountains

I've resorted to hyping up Turnback Canyon so media people will notice us. I hope their attention span is long enough to see past the whitewater and report about what really matters: pipelines and peregrines, mines and moose, Windy Craggy and wilderness. I've written about our Quest in magazines, talked about it on the radio and flogged it in newspapers. Just before we left for the Alsek, I was interviewed by a writer for *National Geographic*. I asked her what it was like to work for the crown prince of magazines.

"I flash my National Geo ID card," she laughed, "and everyone wags their tails like golden retrievers." She sipped coffee in my kitchen and asked me about the Tatshenshini environmental campaign, about acid mine drainage, about the Alsek River. "The photographer will like the Turnback Canyon angle," she said.

This will be my second trip into Turnback Canyon. Eighteen months earlier, Ian, Derek, Rod Leighton and I had tried to become the first Canadian group to kayak it. Halfway through the canyon, we paddled blindly into the jaws of a rapid called "Hair."

Walt Blackadar, a larger-than-life figure in the short history of whitewater kayaking, was the first person to paddle Turnback Canyon. He described Hair in an extravagant article in a 1972 issue of *Sports Illustrated*: "...one huge horrendous mile of hair (the worst foamy rapids a kayaker can imagine). Incredible! I didn't flip in that mile or I wouldn't be writing."

We all flipped in that mile. Some of us several times. Derek had the worst ride—ending with a frightening swim and a lost kayak. Andrew Embick, a kayaker from Alaska had written, "In this canyon, if you swim you die—and Turnback Canyon reeks of death." Derek dispelled that myth and has the dubious distinction of being the only person to survive a swim in Turnback.

Jody was stuck in high school during our first attempt at the canyon. Now he is almost eighteen years old, out of school...and nothing is going to keep him out of our group. Not even his mother has a leash long enough to tether him in town. Joanne Schick is a cheerful woman, but lately she's had a grizzly glint in her eye. Since I don't want to get between Joanne and her cub, I've taken to giving the Schick house a wide berth.

It takes eight days to paddle against a relentless headwind to Turnback Canyon. The canyon, sandwiched between the Tweedsmuir Glacier and the steep flanks of Mt. Blackadar, is one of the most remote spots on earth. The glacier is massive, a frozen whale's back breaching infinitely slowly, filling a broad valley and disappearing into the St. Elias Mountains. The glacier's terminal moraine is surreal, raw and wild, heaps of gravel and stones scoured from mountainsides centuries ago and carried down by flowing ice.

We stake out our tents and tie our tarp to the canoe which serves both as windbreak and storage larder. In a drizzling mist, our tents and tarp are the only splashes of colour. The rest of the world is grey. Jumbled hillocks of rock and gluey silt. Monochrome sky. Across the river, a pair of mountain goats graze on a slate-coloured talus slope.

In the evening, the wind moans over the glacier and icy fingers of rain drum against our tents. We huddle under the tarp in winter attire. Rachel leans against the canoe, reading. She is wearing a down jacket, toque and mitts. She fumbles with her book, shakes off her right mitt and turns the page.

Derek flips on the radio. The reception has been awful and we have given up trying to reach the NorthwesTel operator and CBC. Dirk Freeman though, calls as often as a teenager phoning his steady date. It doesn't take long before we hear, "Alsek Expedition, this is National Geographic. Over."

I grab the microphone. "National Geographic, this is Alsek." I wait a few moments for a reply. "Oh yeah. Over."

"Alsek, I barely copy you. Count to ten. Over."

"One, two...."

"I can't believe Ken's counting to ten again," laughs Jody.

"...nine, ten. Over."

"Okay Alsek. I've got a helicopter lined up for September two-five. What time will you begin paddling? Over."

"Look, we've had tons of rain and the river is too high. We'll have to wait at least a week."

"Say over," says Derek.

"Jesus. *Over.*"

"Man, that's getting tight for time." There's a pause filled with static hiss. "When will you try the canyon? Over."

Dall ram in the Kluane Ranges

"We're hoping for October first. Over."

"Man, that's tight! Okay Alsek, I hear you. October one is our new deadline. I'll check with you again on the evening of September two-seven at 8 o'clock sharp. National Geographic, over and out."

We hang out for several days in steadily deteriorating weather, reading, exploring, lightening our food load. One morning we decide it's time to start portaging the stuff that we can't carry into the canyon with us: the canoe, climbing hardware and spare food. The plan is to hump a load halfway across the glacier and return to camp. Later we'll load up everything except our kayaking gear and set up a new base camp at the bottom of Turnback Canyon. We'll return to our kayaks the day before we run the canyon.

"Looks like a great day to grovel across a glacier with a canoe on your head," jokes Ian. He and Derek lash paddles and ice-axes across the thwarts so two people can balance it on their shoulders.

Rachel, Jody and I each grab a heavy pack. Derek and Ian hoist the canoe. With heads and shoulders scrunched under the boat, they look like a giant cockroach. They scuttle up a shifting slope of moraine and dump the canoe on top. "Your turn," says Ian.

Jody and I lift the canoe. Step, stride, slip. "Hold on, it's sliding off my shoulders." Climb, heave, climb. "Stop for a second. I have to lift the bow to see where the hell we're going." Step, slip, lurch. "Watch out, there's ice just under these boulders. Shit! This is supposed to be a river trip!"

Eventually we reach the clear ice of the Tweedsmuir Glacier. The canoe becomes an ungainly sled. After half a day of hauling we stop, flip it over and slip the packs underneath. I look back as we return across the glacier to camp. The canoe looks absurd, abandoned in an immensity of ice.

The monotonous thudding of rain wakes me the next morning. It's the coldest day yet. I wear mitts all day, except when I'm clutching one of innumerable mugs of coffee. The only exercise I get is darting out from under the tarp to pee. In the evening Dirk Freeman entertains us with his conversational wit. I tell him that insistent rain has kept the water levels high, but it *has* to end soon. Over.

"What do you think the Dirk-Man looks like?" asks Jody after I shut down the radio.

"Glasses, dark hair and a beard," says Rachel.

"I bet he's short and balding," I say. "He'll be wearing a gorky camera-vest and an Australian bush hat."

The next day dawns clear and cold. We dismantle camp and load our backpacks with everything except our kayaking gear. We hike to the shoulder of the glacier. "Listen," says Ian. A "whock-whock-whock" drifts up from the river. A helicopter buzzes up from Turnback Canyon, hovers over our kayaks and swoops towards us like an angry hornet.

The chopper lands on the ice and a man steps from the cockpit. He looks like a page from the latest L.L. Bean catalogue, all leather booted and khakied and wearing a camera vest bristling with pockets and gadgets. He dashes under the whirling rotor blades. He isn't short *or* balding. He looks like Robert Redford.

He strides over, hand extended. "You must be Ken," he says, mashing my hand. "I'm Dirk Freeman. Thought I'd take advantage of the sunshine and fly out here." He shades his eyes and looks across the glacier, assessing f-stops, colour saturation, shutter speeds. "Are you on schedule for October first?"

"Well, this is the first day it hasn't rained all week and the river is still high. We're thinking of the second or third."

"Man, that's tight," says Dirk, his tone sounding as if he's just discovered a slug in his pocket. "My schedule is *tough*. I've been pushing back things. Pushing back things I *need* to do."

"Look, if it stays clear and cold the water might drop by the first, but we're not going to do anything stupid."

"Ach," he groans, "even October first is tight for me, but later than that…damn. Look, I'll radio you the day after tomorrow." He dashes back to the chopper and yells. "Remember! September 30th, eight o'clock sharp." He leans towards the pilot and gestures at Jody and Rachel, who are hiking up the glacier. The helicopter lifts off and circles them, blowing them sideways across the ice.

Unencumbered by the canoe, it is a long but pleasant hike across the glacier to the end of Turnback Canyon.

Derek Endress and Ian portaging across the Tweedsmuir Glacier

Pleasant—until we reach the end of the ice. We struggle to the summit of a mountain of moraine and stare out over a chaos of rock. Fifty square kilometres of moraine. Wave after wave, like something out of the surfing movie *Endless Summer*. Instead of pounding surf though, the waves are hundred foot swells of frozen rock. It is dusk when we stagger to a campsite beside the river.

The sunshine has been heartening, but tonight the stars are dimmed, as if a sheet of waxed paper is stretched tight across the sky. Rain begins in the middle of the night, rain which turns to snow as I cook pancakes the next morning. None of us feels like venturing across the glacier for the stranded canoe and supplies. We kill time under leaking skies, glaring at the river, daring it to rise.

On the last day of September we retrieve the canoe and return for our evening chat with Dirk Freeman. The reception is even fuzzier than usual. He fades in and out but we confirm that October second will be the day. At least I think we confirm it. By the time I finish counting to ten, the audio has deteriorated to plops and hisses, like bubbling porridge.

October first. We can't procrastinate any longer. We wave to Rachel and trudge across the moraine. An even layer of cloud steals across the sky and a thin, cold rain appears. It's hard to tell if the rain is falling or oozing out of the glacier. It's just *there*, part of our world that has shrunk to a few square metres of ice and a mantle of desolate thoughts.

We decide to have a last look at Hair, the touchstone for all my worries about tomorrow. We slither down a vertical granite gully, the rock slick with licorice-coloured mud and wet moss. The river is much higher than last time we were here and the rapid looks awful, right on the edge of what I'm willing to try.

Back at the moraine, we stop to eat. I'm soaked. My fingers are numb and I can't open a zip-lock bag of trail mix. I hand it to Jody. Raindrops splash softly on our jackets. Jody passes back the bag. I stuff a handful of peanuts into my mouth. You know you're on the road to hypothermia when you don't have the energy to pick out extra chocolate chips.

Derek shakes his head gloomily. "It's too high. You shouldn't kayak something like Turnback unless you're feeling confident. I just didn't paddle enough this year. I don't want to be a liability."

"It's your call," says Ian. "But don't worry about being a liability. We're all in this together."

I can't think of anything to say that isn't trivial. We put away the food and hike through the fog to our kayaks. Jody props up the tarp using his paddle as a centre-pole, arranging the edges so rainwater won't soak our sleeping bags.

"I'm going to portage the first half of the canyon," says Derek. "I'm pretty sure I can lower the kayak down to the water somewhere below Hair."

"Sounds like a good idea," I say. At the same time I'm questioning my own motives, wondering what is driving me on. Ego? The quest for publicity? We crawl into our sleeping bags to stay warm.

When I was a kid, I had a recurring nightmare about a lion. It has been thirty years since the beast has stalked my sleep, but it comes again tonight. I sprint down a path with a friend on my heels. I can't see who he is. The lion chases us with great leaps. At a fork in the trail I turn one way, my friend the other. The lion's muscles look like pistons beneath its tawny coat. It pounces on my friend. I hear a scream.

I sit up in my sleeping bag. It's pitch black. All I can hear is the patter of rain and the throb of the Alsek. Shit. My gloomiest thoughts are invading my sleep. For some bizarre psychological reason I never imagine that I'll get hurt, but I worry about my friends. I toss and turn until Derek's watch buzzes at dawn.

The stove is strategically placed so Jody can boil water without emerging from his sleeping bag. "Coffee's ready," he says after a few minutes. It's thick and black, like motor oil. I stir in a heaping spoonful of brown sugar.

Derek crawls into the early morning light. "I'm out of here. Good luck." His footsteps clatter on the stones.

I dawdle in my sleeping bag. My skin wants to stay warm. My bladder wants the relentless pressure eased. The bladder wins. Steam rises from the urine splashing on the rocks.

I wander over to my kayak and stuff in my sleeping bag. Ian dumps granola from a plastic bag into our mugs, and we spoon in powdered milk and glacial meltwater. The milk refuses to dissolve in the frigid water. Custard-white lumps float to the surface like blobs of algae in a swamp. I force my jaws to chew while we finish loading our kayaks. I'm pulling

Ian packing his kayak before paddling Turnback Canyon

my dry suit over my head when the helicopter drops from the sky.

Dirk, Bart Henderson and the pilot jump out of the chopper. Bart runs a rafting business in Haines, Alaska. Today he's Dirk's servant. Dirk bustles around importantly, waving his arms and talking about shooting locations and camera angles. They remove the door, unload spare fuel drums and vibrate into the sky. We slide into the river.

↗   ↗   ↗

The "S-bends" are the first rapids, a series of tight turns between sheer rock walls. This is where the French kayaker drowned a decade ago. He was young, just a little older than Jody is now. I wonder if Jody is thinking about him. I'm nervous. My kayak should be an extension of my body, but I feel sloppy after several weeks in a canoe. The water is cold. Burning cold. Numbing cold. None of us is brave enough to practice an Eskimo roll.

The river screams over the horizon line at the first big rapid. It's hard to see a route, and it is impossible to get out of our boats to scout. I glance at Jody and Ian, shrug my shoulders and take off. I plunge down a tongue of current beside a huge "hole"—a maelstrom of foaming water capable of stopping, thrashing and recirculating a kayaker.

"All right!" I yell as Jody and Ian blast through. I'm happy that the first rapid is behind us. We surf in front of an undercut wall, zip around a corner...and run into the helicopter, hovering like a mutant dragonfly above the river. Dirk, windblown and handsome, is tethered by a harness and hanging out the door.

The helicopter is doing its best to create a rapid where one doesn't exist. I paddle hard, but the wind flings me into a boil. I brace and escape downriver while Dirk turns his attention to the others.

"That thing is totally gross," yells Jody after the chopper whirrs downriver.

We climb out of our kayaks above a difficult rapid named Dyna-flow. Bart is standing on shore. "Where's the helicopter?" asks Ian.

"It's refuelling. Dirk is set up below the rapid."

"Hey Bart," I say, "could you ask the pilot to stay higher? The down-draft blasted us back there."

I pull my camera out of a dry-bag while Ian and Jody climb across a ledge to scout. They are contemplating a hideous hole at the end of the rapid when I join them.

"Most of the water is going left of the hole," says Jody, gesturing at the river. "I'm going to be in the middle, paddling hard left after those standing waves." Ian nods in agreement. They walk to their kayaks, looking back at the rapid as they go, charting their route. Jody's voice floats back before his words are deadened by the roar of whitewater. "It wouldn't be much fun in the hole."

I extend the legs on my tripod, wedge it onto a sloping ledge and snap the camera onto the head. Ian goes first. He rollercoasters over the waves and paddles hard left—too hard. A boil mushrooms from the wall and spins him around. Fortunately, Ian is an authority on the art of running rapids backwards. He balances on a tightrope of water and rockets downstream.

Jody breaks out of the eddy, his long red kayak slashing through the waves. He's right on line, looking good, when an exploding wave swallows him. One moment he's there—then he's a reddish blur under the surface. I barely have time to look up from my camera before he's flushing past the hole, still submerged. Ian, who is sitting in an eddy just below Dirk, waves his paddle, signalling that Jody is okay.

I slide into the river as the helicopter scoops up Bart. It moves slowly downstream and hovers directly above Dynaflow. Its down-draft whips up spray that rebounds from the cliffs and rises like steam. I wave my paddle and point upwards. The helicopter rises a few metres, but there is no difference in the flying mist. I'm too embarrassed to point again, so I nose into the current.

As I skirt a pair of holes, a blast of spray blinds me. My kayak stalls as it crests a breaking wave, then the helicopter hurricane lifts my bow and blows me *upstream*, back into the trough of the wave. I close my eyes and lean forward. I dig my paddle into the current and haul the kayak over the wave. When I pass under the chopper, I'm blown through the slot as explosively as a cork from a bottle of cheap champagne.

Dirk is packing away his camera when I join Jody and Ian. "Look," I shout, "the chopper is going to have to stay

The rapid known as "Hair"

higher off the deck." His forehead wrinkles in protest...then he looks at my face and nods.

We turn our boats downriver, scouting from our kayaks. Dark, brooding rock walls slide upstream, mirroring my mood. I'm out of touch with the river, caught up in the whirl of rotor blades. We squirt through a slot beside a huge pillar of rock.

"Hair is just around the corner," yells Ian.

My hands tingle as though sparks of nervous energy are jumping from finger to finger. This is the crux of the canyon and I need to focus, fast. I concentrate on breathing deeply, breathing evenly, one deep breath after another. Suddenly everything slows down. It feels as if I'm above the river where I can see a clear route through the jumbled waves. I reach into a wall of white that breaks over my head. I'm underwater but still upright, my paddle blade braced in the strong current.

By the time I find an eddy and look upstream, Jody is past the worst. A few seconds later Ian zooms into view, slams his bow into the cliff and slides backwards down the chute. He braces wildly, then spins and paddles casually into the eddy. Tension hisses from my body like air from a punctured balloon.

Derek and Dirk are standing on a bluff, packing up their cameras. We wave, paddle through a boily rapid and beach our boats. The helicopter picks up Dirk and settles down on a cliff-top across the river.

"Yeah," yells Derek as he climbs towards us, "good paddling!"

"Hey, yeah!" says Jody. "Where's your boat?"

"I left it up at the moraine. I wanted to get down here in time to take pictures of you in Hair."

"I'm starving," I say. "Let's eat and then get your boat." Across the river the helicopter is quiet, but I can feel Dirk staring at us.

"I can't believe that Dirk," says Derek. "I told him it would take an hour to carry my kayak down. He asked if I knew how much it cost to rent a helicopter. He said you guys should leave me behind. He thought I'd solo the rest of the canyon to suit his busy schedule."

"No way," says Jody through a mouthful of stoned wheat and Gouda. "Hey Ken, chuck me that chocolate."

"I told him how things work out here," says Derek.

It takes 90 minutes to scramble up the rock bands and

retrieve Derek's kayak. I can feel the weight of Dirk's impatience from across the river—impatience to the tune of $750 per hour of helicopter time.

After paddling through a boily slot called the "Percolator," there is just one big rapid left. We jostle into a tiny eddy to scout, pull our kayaks onto the rocks and clamber onto a ledge.

"Look," says Ian, "we should be on the other side." Across the river there's a line of waves. Big, but manageable. Unfortunately, we can't get there. On this side, our choice is a twisting slot or a ten-foot falls. Dirk's 600 mm Nikon lens is aimed in our direction. I imagine him tapping his feet, looking at his watch. We dither for 20 minutes.

"Look at that seam," says Jody finally. "If you ferry across *there*, you could make it into the main flow. But watch out for that monster hole."

"I know what *I'm* doing," says Derek, pointing at the shore. "I'm carrying my boat around." It's a sensible idea, but the rest of us are reluctant to portage after paddling this far. We decide to try Jody's route.

Jody steadies my boat while I get in. I slide into the current, fighting to maintain the correct angle of boat against water. I tuck my bow behind a boulder and squirm through a rock garden. A breaking wave upends me, and I spin downstream, my kayak vertical, my body buried in the water. I regain control just above the hole and retreat to shore.

I catch my breath and look upstream. Jody looks tiny in the huge river. He's paddling backwards, looking over his shoulder at the hole. He digs in his paddle and surfs to the opposite shore.

"Pretty wild stuff," says a voice. It's the helicopter pilot, squatting above me on the rocks, smoking a cigarette. "Hey, your buddy's in shit!"

Ian is upside-down, floating towards the jaws of the hole. It pulses with spray, as if salivating, anticipating a meal. Ian's paddle beats the surface as he tries to roll, again and again. Fortunately, a curling wave flings him to one side of the hole. He rolls up on his fifth attempt, red-faced, eyes bulging.

"Shee-it," says the pilot. "Doesn't look like fun to me. Well,

Ian demonstrates the art of paddling backwards in Turnback Canyon

I guess the boss will be ready to go." He flicks his cigarette into the eddy where it lands with a hiss and a puff of steam. "No way you'd get me out there." He walks back to the helicopter.

I fish the butt out of the river and drop it in the pouch in the front of my dry suit. It joins assorted bits of foil, candy wrappers and a dripping lighter that is supposed to be waterproof. I paddle down to the others who are out of their boats, looking over the next rapid.

The helicopter roars over us, heading back towards civilization. A fist pokes out the door, raised in a "power to the people" salute. "Looks like Dirk shot enough blood and guts action in the last rapid," says Ian.

The racket of the helicopter dissipates, its last vibrations absorbed by the ice and rock. It takes longer for my ears to stop quivering. We want the photographs, we want the media attention...but I'm glad the damn thing is gone. Why is nothing ever simple? Why do we need to import 1990s hype in a bid to convince people thousands of kilometres away that the mountains shouldn't be levelled? That the rivers shouldn't be poisoned?

I can hear the river again. I feel the wind in my face. I see a dark speck soaring above the canyon downstream. The wilderness washes over me, like the return of night vision after staring at a bright light.

We ride over a series of standing waves and squirt through the last constriction in the canyon. I lean back on my stern deck and look up. The speck is now a bald eagle, wings outstretched, circling. I gesture to my friends with my paddle. We're silent, as if afraid that we've already presumed too much by inviting the helicopter out here, as if our voices will be too much of an intrusion now.

We float with the current for a few minutes. Jody points towards the bank. I see a glistening thread of meltwater from an ice field and then three motionless shapes, a sow grizzly and a pair of cubs. They look sleek and healthy, almost ready to crawl into a den for the winter. Their senses are no doubt assaulted by our colour, shape and scent—as we were by the rattle and stench of the chopper.

They watch as the river sweeps us around the corner and out of sight.

KIDS
ON THE ALSEK

The early June breeze filters through the window, ruffling curtains and spinning the whale mobile. Cardboard orcas, humpbacks and grey whales swim lazily over the crib as I plop Malcolm on his quilt. It's nine o'clock. Bedtime. But the low-angle Yukon sunshine is oozing as thick as honey between cracks in the curtains and I wonder if I'll be able to cajole Malcolm to sleep.

"Tell me a story," he says, clinging to my sleeve with pudgy but determined fingers, "a story about a moose."

"Malcolm," I say firmly, "I just read you a story, and so did Wendy."

"I want a story about a moose."

I'm tired. In the summer, northerners don't have time for mundane pursuits like sleeping. The dark days of winter are gone, hiding out somewhere in southern Chile and it seems ridiculous to go to sleep when the sun is still shining hotly. Earlier, while brushing Malcolm's teeth, I had looked in the mirror. My eyes looked bleary, vacant, as if I'd just finished an eight-hour shift at Canadian Tire.

"Okay, just one story. This is a story about the river trip we're going on tomorrow. Now, what is your middle name?"

"Malcolm."

"No, your next name."

"Alsek."

"That's right. Well, Malcolm Alsek was floating down the Alsek River. He paddled and paddled and saw lots of animals. Dall sheep played on the mountain sides. Mountain goats watched Malcolm from a steep cliff. Beavers slapped their tails and swam under the raft. A bald eagle...."

"What about a moose?"

"I'm getting to that. Malcolm camped one night in the spruce trees near the river. He was snoring in his tent when he suddenly woke up. There was a loud noise in the forest. Thump, thump, thump. It got nearer and nearer. Malcolm wriggled his arms out of his sleeping bag and slowly unzipped the tent. Then he stuck his nose outside and bumped into an animal with humungous antlers. What do you think it was?"

Malcolm Alsek Boothroyd with moose antler beside the Alsek River

"A moose," breathes Malcolm.

"That's right," I say, rubbing his hair, "and if we're lucky, we'll see a real moose on our trip. Okay, have a good sleep little guy. I love you."

"Is a moose a bad aminal?" His voice sounds small.

"No, they are wild animals, but they aren't bad. Good night."

I walk past the kitchen table piled high with plastic bags of pasta, pesto and parmesan. The green shag rug in the living room is heaped with long underwear, sleeping bags...and eight pairs of pants for Malcolm. Our house is a chaos of trip preparation, but I want to forget about it for a few minutes. I grab an escapist novel and try to lose myself in the steamy summer streets of San Francisco.

"Is Malcolm sleeping?" asks my partner, Wendy Boothroyd.

"Not yet."

"A moose," wails a voice, a fully awake voice. "A mooo-oose."

"What's the matter?" I say irritably, stomping to his room. "I just told you a moose story."

"A moose is coming in my room!"

"Listen, don't worry. Moose don't come inside people's houses."

"I want Wendy. I don't want a moose in my room! We-e-endy."

Forty minutes and a dozen visits to his room later he is still crying and hiccuping miserably. I stagger out and collapse on the green shag.

This trip is supposed to be a celebration—my first trip into the Alsek watershed since the government of British Columbia quashed plans for the Windy Craggy mine and designated the new Tatshenshini-Alsek Wilderness Park. Wendy was pregnant with Malcolm when we paddled down the Tatshenshini during our Wilderness Quest. Now Malcolm is two, and it's time to baptize him in the watershed for which he was named.

There *has* to be symbolism in bringing Malcolm along. After all, during the Tatshenshini campaign, we environmentalists repeated with single-minded piousness that we need to preserve wilderness for generations to come. The time has come. A chance for the next generation to toss

27

rocks in the river, drool on the beach and rub its nose in the silt. A chance for the next generation to take the first steps toward feeling a responsibility to care for wildlands.

But I'm worried. Not about safety. Not about rapids or foul weather or bears. I'm worried by my own selfishness. River trips are a chance to get away from the hoops I leap through at society's bidding. A chance to leave behind shopping malls and cars and the stock market quotations on the radio. We aren't leaving Malcolm behind though. I've never dealt with a small child in the backcountry before.

In nine hours we're taking off for a week-long trip, and Malcolm is still screaming about a moose in his bedroom.

∕   ∕   ∕

"What kind of animals do you think we'll see on the river?" asks Juri Peepre, glancing over his shoulder at his three-year-old son Alex. I'm in the back seat with a pack on my lap, jammed between a pair of car seats. Juri, his partner Sarah Locke, and Wendy are squeezed in front.

"*I* think we're going to see whales," shouts Alex.

"That would be cool," I say, "but don't whales live in salt water?"

The dirt road snakes through fields of saxifrage. The hillsides are terraced rock gardens blooming with Jacob's ladder, cinqfoil and hedysarum. It wasn't a Paul Bunyan of a gardener who raked out these terraces, but the wave action of lakes formed by the Lowell Glacier, 50 kilometres downstream.

Glaciers normally plod slowly down from high elevation snowfields, but occasionally they gallop. It's called surging. The Lowell Glacier has surged several times in the last few centuries, crossing the Alsek and jamming up against the solid rock flanks of Goatherd Mountain. The ice-dams would have been the envy of the U.S. Army Corps of Engineers. When the river finally ruptured the dam, the floodwaters were many times the volume of the Amazon, a giant wall of water that wiped out aboriginal villages at the Tatshenshini confluence and on the coast at Dry Bay.

Maybe the glacier will surge again. If the river ever backs

Upper Alsek River landscape

up as high as it did in 1853, you'll need scuba gear to get to the Kluane National Park visitors' centre in the town of Haines Junction.

We jostle over a rise and the Alsek Valley stretches out below us, spacious, wide open, scoured by the floods when ice-dams collapsed. "Look," says Wendy, "in a few hours we'll be floating down that river."

"Let's throw salt in the water," yells Alex. "Then the whales will swim up to us."

We drive down to a rocky beach and unload our gear on the gravel. The river is placid, like a sleeping child that gives no hint of its potential for causing trouble. The winds also are calm, unusually calm for a valley that often acts as a wind tunnel for storms searching for the easiest route through the St. Elias Mountains.

We've decided to use a raft for this trip, reasoning that the kids will be able to crawl around without compromising stability. Our raft is an ancient craft called the Sag Stallion that has more scars and skin grafts than Evel Knievel. We also have a stubby Topolino kayak in which the adults can take turns playing.

We pump up the raft and pile in our gear...including a diaper pail, teddy bears and plastic pails and shovels. It's a warm June day with only a few cumulus clouds playing lazily in a sky that seems bleached by the sun. I watch the shifting pattern of shadows on the slopes, relieved to be out of the car, happy to be on the river. Wendy takes the first shift in the kayak and Juri, Sarah and I pretend that our paddle strokes are actually moving the heavily-laden Sag Stallion. We drift sluggishly downstream.

"When are we going to get dere?" asks Malcolm.

"There isn't much current until the Kaskawulsh River comes in," I explain, "so we want to get a few kilometres downstream before the wind picks up."

"When are we going to get dere?"

"Maybe you guys are getting hungry," says Juri enthusiastically. "How about some crackers?" He opens a dry bag, digs around and pulls out a box of Stoned Wheat Thins. "Hey that's funny! The box is crushed already." He hands Malcolm a chunk of cracker. "Here Alex, have some crackers."

"I don't want a piece of cracker," says Alex. "I want a whole one."

"Alex, on trips sometimes crackers get broken, but they taste just the same."

"I want a whole one."

"I'm taking them off the top, Alex," explains Juri patiently, "once we get past the broken ones we can eat the whole ones."

"I don't want a broken one," Alex says with an escalating whine. "I *told* you I want a whole one."

We lurch downstream into a slough-like widening of the river. A light headwind ruffles the water—light, but enough to slow our progress to a crawl. Wendy floats peacefully ahead, out of whining range. Malcolm squirms over the heap of packs to the stern of the raft and tries to wriggle onto my lap.

"You can sit next to me," I say, "but I can't paddle if you are on top of me." He looks up at me with youthful innocence. Then he punches me on the arm. "Malcolm, please don't hit me." He slugs me again. "*No*, Malcolm!" As he cocks his arm for another swing I toss the paddle into the raft and grab his hand, but the paddle rebounds off the rubbery floor and smacks him on the chin.

"*Wendy*," shrieks Malcolm. "I want Wendy."

We head for shore.

I tie the Sag Stallion to a sturdy willow. We chuck the gear onto shore and put up the tents in a meadow. Sarah and Juri volunteer to cook supper, so Wendy and I round up the kids for a hike. There is no need to look for a trail, the hillsides are wide open, more a desert landscape than a boreal forest. Rock and sand with widely scattered spruce and low-lying juniper. I take a deep breath, stretching my arms out so my lungs can suck in as much brisk air as possible.

"Isn't this great?" I say. "Just look at those mountains."

"These are our guns, right Malcolm?" says Alex. The kids are looking down, not up. They have sticks and are poking vigorously at an ant hill.

"Hey you guys," says Wendy virtuously, "ants are animals. This is their *home*. How would you like it if a giant ant shoved a stick into your house?"

Alex Peepre and Malcolm turn themselves into muck monsters

"Let's kill the ants," says Malcolm.

"Forget it," I say. "You can't play with sticks if you disturb natural things." Wendy and I each grab an arm and hustle them back towards camp.

"Look," says Malcolm excitedly. "Moose poop! Let's take some home."

The cylindrical pellets are dried, about the size of my thumb. A few years ago, moose droppings were a growth industry in the north. Entrepreneurs believe that everything has economic value. Even moose shit. Why else would God leave it lying around? They'd collect sackfuls, shellac them, attach wings and snouts, and presto—moosequitos. They'd put in pink plastic sticks and make moose swizzle sticks. They'd use the pellets as the baubles on Australian bush hats. Tourists will buy anything.

Malcolm and Alex each grab a handful and shove it into their pockets. I'm hoping that Malcolm isn't old enough to make the connection that moose poop comes from a moose. And a moose is a wild animal. And Malcolm doesn't want a moose in his bedroom, or his tent. I need some sleep tonight.

When we return, the fixings for a tortilla meal are spread out between a pair of spruce trees: a mug filled with shredded cheese, bowls of tomatoes and onions, a pot of refried beans that looks like sauteed moose poop. A wisp of smoke curls up from the small bed of coals on the fire-pan. It's a picnic scene from *Better Homes and Gardens* until Malcolm decides to visit the log that has become Alex's chair.

"Stay away from the fire," warns Wendy as Malcolm weaves into the kitchen area. He looks like a drunk in a spaghetti western, lurching out of a saloon. Except he's clutching a dripping tortilla instead of a six-shooter. Wendy moves to block his route towards the fire, so he staggers into the dutch oven, upends the mug of cheese and kicks dirt onto my plate.

"Just about bedtime!" I say with exaggerated cheerfulness. "You can play for a few more minutes while we clean up after supper." Malcolm and Alex build castles with pine cones and rocks while we rinse the dishes and carry the food away from camp. The trees are too spindly to be useful for bear-proofing our supplies. Wilderness bears seldom raid camps, but if it should happen, we'd rather they have their feast well away from our tents.

"Don't even think about mentioning the moose word," I whisper to Wendy as we haul Malcolm to the tent to diaper and pyjama him.

"Time to brush your teeth," I say, waving a loaded toothbrush in front of Malcolm's face. "Okay, spit." A blob that looks like guano dribbles over his chin and oozes down his sleeper. I dab at the spittle on his chest with my sleeve, grab him around the waist and pass him to Wendy like a sack of potatoes. "Sleeping in a tent is fun!"

It is fun for Malcolm, but sleep is not on his agenda. "Read me a story," he demands. We've brought along two books, *Green Eggs and Ham* and *Curious George*. I read in a soothing, monotone voice, hoping to bore him to sleep. But he's out of his sleeping bag and wriggling as soon as I close the cover on George and the man with the yellow hat.

"Please don't play with the zipper," says Wendy. "Just lay down with your teddies and relax. *Malcolm!* Don't pull my hair!"

After an hour or so he stops twitching and breathes evenly. Wendy and I lay rigidly, willing him to drop off to sleep. Then, from the tent across the meadow we hear "No more stories," and a high-pitched, unintelligible squawk.

Malcolm lifts his head. "Is that Alex?"

The next morning it begins to rain. In the raft, Juri dredges up songs from his Ontario summer camp youth. It has been a long time since I've heard "The Ants Go Marching," "Puff the Magic Dragon," and "99 Bottles of Beer on the Wall." The drizzle looks like it is settling in so we look for a place to stop after a couple of hours on the water.

We camp beside a deep back eddy flanked by hills of ancient lava. Rainwater drips from alders. A dozen paces from our tent and we could be in Utah, all arid rock dotted with enormous granite boulders. The boulders are known as "erratics." They were dropped off by retreating glaciers after the latest ice age. Malcolm and Alex aren't interested in geography. They are playing beside the river, turning themselves into muck monsters.

I had thought that bringing eight pairs of pants for Malcolm was overkill, but by the time the sun finally comes out thirty-six hours later, seven pairs are saturated with mud, stained

Iceberg in Lowell Lake

with pesto or sopping with urine. We declare a laundry day at the next campsite. Every branch and bush becomes a drying rack, littered with overalls, diapers and socks. It looks like a shantytown on the outskirts of Mexico City.

"When everyone was looking the other way, Malcolm and Alex jumped out of the raft. The water was magic, and before you could say Moose Poop, they turned into beavers."

We've been out for five days and the raft is floating through country at least as magical as the story I'm telling. Deep emerald pools in the lava. Young cliff swallows in mud nests on rock walls. Steely blue glaciers. As the Alsek cuts closer to the heart of the St. Elias Mountains the peaks crowd closer to the river, as if they too want to hear the story.

"What did the beavers do?" asks Malcolm.

"They swam under the raft and hid. And then Sarah said, 'Hey, what happened to Alex and Malcolm?' Everyone looked over the edge, so the young beavers swam to the other side and whacked their tails on the river. They splashed so much water that the raft filled up. When the water touched Sarah and Wendy and Juri and Ken, they turned into beavers too. And they lived happily ever after."

"Tell another story about Alex and Malcolm Beaver," says Alex, but the river is speeding up and there are waves ahead. All the Alsek's big rapids are below the Lowell Glacier, but we don't want to take the kids through even mild whitewater. We carry them overland and take turns paddling the kayak and raft into the widening of the river called Lowell Lake. Then we haul our gear over the rubble left behind by the glacier. We put up our tents near a flat stretch of moraine that doubles as an airstrip for bushpilots.

"What do you think of this moraine?" I ask Wendy.

"Moraine is gross."

"Come on Wendy. You have to admit this is beautiful."

"No. I don't."

We have this conversation off and on. During Wendy's seventh month of pregnancy I asked her what she thought of the name Moraine for a girl. Wendy said it made her think of shifting rubble, gluey muck and days of portaging around Turnback Canyon. She said the name made her hope the kid was a boy. Moraine. I think it's a nice name.

33

The next day we take turns hiking up Goatherd Mountain. The ice-polished rock is entwined with bands of yellow and gold. The meadows are covered with flowers: moss campion, prickly saxifrage and mountain avens. Mountain goats pick their way across the precipitous face of the mountain. Below them is a thousand metre drop to the moraine and the iceberg-filled lake.

While Wendy and Sarah are hiking, Juri and I decide to walk down to Lowell Lake with the kids. As we near the water we stumble over an Arctic tern's nest filled with delicate white eggs peppered with brown blotches. The tern flies with jerky wingbeats, dive bombing us if we get too close. The lake is a menagerie of icebergs calved from the face of the glacier. There are ducks, dwarves, sea-serpents and a frog with a gaping mouth. There are electric blue icebergs 20 metres high and tiny ones, translucent and sparkling.

Small chunks of ice jostle in the breeze near shore but the kids wade in, oblivious to the cold. It's idyllic: kids playing in the water, Mt. Kennedy in the distance, the thunderous booming of calving icebergs.

"Let's have a Lowell egg hunt," says Juri. "Close your eyes and I'll hide these chocolates."

Alex and Malcolm count to ten, then race along the shore. Alex finds one immediately and inhales it. Malcolm wanders in a circle, looking stunned, while Alex pounces on the second. I'm braced for a scene, but Alex surprises me.

"Malcolm, look over here," yells Alex. "Here's yours!"

The kids have been model citizens all day. No whining. No deliberately squashing bugs. No paranoia, even when we discovered fresh grizzly tracks near our tents in the morning. Now they are sharing chocolate! Weird.

Maybe they are settling into the wilderness scene. It always takes me a few days to shrug off the stresses of civilization at the beginning of a trip. Maybe it's the same for them. Now I wish the plane wasn't coming this afternoon and we could live out here a little longer.

The breeze turns into a wind by noon, then a gale. It stirs up giant streamers of silt that look like shimmering heat waves. Malcolm is sleepy so I cradle him on my lap and lean

Alex with his parents above the Alsek River

(right) Rainbow beside the Alsek River

against a rock. He snores gently, feeling warm against my chest. The fine sand swirls around us, finding its way down my shirt and into my socks. There is a layer of silt on Malcolm's cheek and a sand dune inside his ear. If we sat here for much longer, we'd be completely covered, just another hump in the moraine.

After Malcolm wakes up, I carry him over to where the others are waiting for the plane, in the lee of a giant, rectangular boulder. Malcolm and Alex pick up pieces of driftwood and disappear behind the boulder while I tell Wendy and Sarah about Alex sharing the chocolate down at the lake. I don't know what they're thinking, but I'm impressed by the way the kids have *grown* out here. Maybe the wilderness will help shape their characters, like the immense glacial forces have shaped this land.

We hear the drone of the plane, a deep hum against the howl of the wind. Then vigorous whacking noises come from behind the boulder. "What are those guys doing?" asks Wendy.

"These are our axes, right, Malcolm?" says Alex. "We're loggers, right?"

"Let's chop down these trees," says Malcolm, pulling the leaves from a young willow and hacking it with a piece of driftwood.

It shouldn't be funny, but we can't help laughing. We'll talk to them about defoliating the shrubbery later. Before the next trip.

The Stikine Watershed

The Stikine Watershed

The B.C. Ministry of Parks' office in the town of Dease Lake is classic northern highway architecture—a mobile home with a green shack tacked on as an office. The only thing missing is a pair of moose antlers nailed over the door. A beefy man with black hair and a moustache pokes his head out of the office. He looks like someone who left the city so he could wear jeans and a lumberjack shirt to work.

"I remember you from last year," he says. "You're kayakers, right?"

Jody and I had driven to Dease Lake, a town of a few hundred people on the Stewart-Cassiar Highway, twice the previous autumn. We were headed for the Grand Canyon of the Stikine after canoeing the upper river, but we never made it to the water. The first time a prolonged downpour swelled the Stikine to suicidal high-water conditions. We hastily called our friend Sue Johnson. She motored down from Whitehorse with sea kayaks and the three of us paddled the lower Stikine to Wrangell. We hoped that the flood waters would subside during the trip.

Two weeks later Jody and I returned to Dease Lake to find that an early winter storm had blanketed the Stikine Plateau with snow. Rafts of mushy ice floated down the river. We scurried back to Whitehorse to exchange our kayaks for skis. We may not be smart, but we're persistent. It's a year later, September 1993, and now we're back.

The Parks official ushers us into his office. He sinks into a swivel chair, puts his hands across his stomach and stares at us with fatherly concern. I can tell we are about to be "Officially Warned." The B.C. Ministry of Parks has declared the Grand Canyon of the Stikine a "recreation area." He's sure it's his duty to keep tabs on what goes on there.

"I hope you're not planning to try the Grand Canyon again."

"We wouldn't think of it," I answer flippantly.

He stares at me as though he's the high school principal and I've just let off a stink bomb in the girls' bathroom. "You know that it's my job to discourage you."

"Go ahead, but you're not going to change our minds."

(previous pages) Coastal rainforest beside the lower Stikine

Jody sea kayaking down the lower Stikine

"I suppose you think you know what you're in for."
We nod.

"I have to ask you this. What makes guys like you do this crazy stuff?"

I know that if someone asks that question, he wouldn't understand the answer, but I fumble for something to say. "Well, an adventure like this can be almost overwhelming, but there are sharp moments when you really know you're alive."

"Or dead," he says sternly.

Baring my soul won't work. I can't even explain to myself why I get an obsession to try something like the Stikine. I try a trite conversation-stopper. "I'd rather die on the Stikine than out on the highway, flattened by a truck."

"At least most people don't go looking for it."

I shrug and we leave it at that. He writes down our names, addresses and dates of birth so he can notify our next of kin.

The Stikine begins as a drip of meltwater in northern B.C.'s Skeena Mountains. It flows through Spatsizi Plateau Wilderness Park, thunders through its Grand Canyon and pierces the glaciated world of the Coast Mountains before emptying into the Pacific Ocean near Wrangell, Alaska. Its watershed—encompassing six life zones or biogeoclimatic

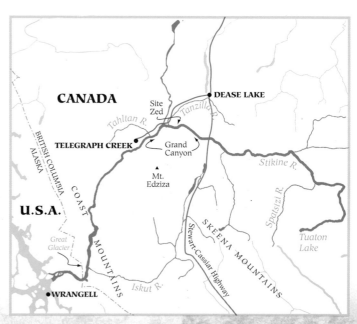

zones—ranges from alpine tundra in the mountains to rain forest in the Boundary Ranges.

I've been intrigued by the Stikine since 1977, when I drove north to teach in a two-room school near Cassiar, B.C. From the metal deck of the highway bridge, I watched the broad, silty Stikine flowing westward. No one had yet tried to kayak the Grand Canyon. It was a place of mystery even to locals.

The first attempts to paddle the canyon were in 1981 and 1985. These trips were supported by helicopters and financed by television companies. The film footage gave the Stikine a reputation as one of the most dangerous rivers in the world. In 1989, an expert kayaker nearly drowned in Entry Falls, the first rapid. It wasn't until 1990 that three Americans—Rob Lesser, Doug Ammons and Tom Schibig—managed to travel the length of the canyon without helicopter support.

No Canadians had paddled the Grand Canyon, and there was no record of anyone travelling the entire Stikine, from its headwaters to the Pacific. Remote whitewater has a magnetic fascination for both Jody and me, but whitewater tells only a fragment of a watershed's story. We wanted to experience the whole river. We decided to canoe the upper Stikine, kayak the Grand Canyon and sea-kayak to the coast.

The upper Stikine is a popular wilderness canoeing river, a ten-day journey from the alpine tundra down through old-growth boreal forest. The Stikine's headwaters are famous for wildlife, including woodland caribou, stone sheep, wolves, raptors and owls. The river is mostly placid, although paddlers find occasional rapids and at least one portage.

Below the Stewart-Cassiar Highway, the only road to cross the Stikine, the river changes character. The 100-kilometre-long Grand Canyon of the Stikine is Canada's largest chasm with dazzling sedimentary cliffs and an underlying bedrock gorge. Unless you are one of the hundreds of mountain goats who are comfortable on canyon walls, most of it is accessible only by confronting absurdly difficult rapids.

The lower Stikine is a powerful watercourse of swirling silt. Salmon swim up to spawn in the lower reaches of the Grand Canyon. For centuries grizzlies and bald eagles have shared the fish harvest with indigenous people: the Tahltans who lived in the interior, and the coastal Tlingits. John Muir

Telegraph Creek

travelled up the lower Stikine in 1879 and called it "a Yosemite 100 miles long."

The Great River. That's what the Tlingits called the Stikine. The name fits. The watershed has held on to its wild nature and shrugged off the worst excesses of developers who try to convert the natural world into rising quotations on the New York and Toronto stock exchanges.

A bizarre series of entrepreneurial assaults in the watershed began with the fur traders, soon followed by a gold rush in the 1860s. Western Union then decided to link New York and Paris by telegraph—via Siberia, the Bering Strait and the Stikine. A sternwheeler had just steamed up to Telegraph Creek with a shipment of wire when the trans-Atlantic cable was completed and the project collapsed.

The lower Stikine was a historic trading corridor for the Tlingits and Tahltans. In 1898, thousands of Klondike gold stampeders laboured up the Stikine, trudged over trails to the Yukon River system and rafted to Dawson City. In 1900, Dawson was linked to the rest of the world via a telegraph line that crossed the Stikine at Telegraph Creek.

A rough road was hacked from Telegraph Creek to Dease Lake in 1928 and the Stikine became a supply line to the interior. The completion of the Stewart-Cassiar Highway in 1969 stifled the Stikine's future as a major transportation link.

During the 1970s, the B.C. government threw tens of millions of dollars into two ill-fated mega-projects. B.C. Rail planned to "open the wealth of the North" with an extension linking Fort St. James with Dease Lake. Not long before the project imploded they spent three million dollars on a bridge across the Stikine just east of the highway—a bridge that goes nowhere and has never carried a train.

B.C. Hydro's mega-vision was a five-dam hydroelectric complex. Ironically, if both this project and the railway extension had gone ahead, the reservoir created up by the dams in the Grand Canyon would have submerged the railway bridge. Plans to dam the Stikine are temporarily gone, but not forgotten.

People who care about the Stikine are bewildered about how to fight a myriad of new development proposals for the watershed—mining, logging and road building. The Great River will need all the help it can get to ensure that it doesn't turn into a tamed slough like the Columbia.

A LEGEND OF THE UPPER STIKINE

"Hold on to your stomachs," says the pilot, "there's weather out there." I glance at Sue Johnson, my paddling partner for the upper Stikine. Sue is crammed into the back of the Cessna 185. Her face is moon-pale, her smile grim. She looks nauseated.

"The canoe still there?" asks the pilot with a malicious grin, watching as I peer out the plexiglass window at the canoe lashed to the struts. "You hear about the canoe that fell off a Cessna south of Atlin? Amazing it didn't take a wing or a tail with it." I check again, inspecting the knots with a critical eye.

Down below, the Stewart-Cassiar Highway is a brown scar scratched across the boreal forest. Dust balloons behind a recreational vehicle bouncing south. It is late August, time for the winter migration of Canada geese, trumpeter swans, sandhill cranes...and tourists.

A couple of centuries ago, only a few restless white people willingly left civilization behind and travelled to the north. A special breed of person, a Samuel Hearne or an Alexander MacKenzie. Now anyone can do it. Simply slap a second mortgage on the cottage, head to the nearest recreational vehicle (RV) dealer and wheel towards the Arctic in a 10,000 kilogram metal and plastic womb.

In early summer, tourists pile into RVs with names like "Freedom," "Columbus" or "Wilderness Traveller" and jostle towards Alaska in an endless stream. To ease the shock of leaving home they bring along the essentials: microwave ovens, blenders, video games, stereo systems, reclining chairs and televisions wired to satellite dishes.

Technological advances insulate us from the environment, both physically and spiritually. My tent shelters me from the rain; but in a Winnebago, with the thermostat cranked up and the television tuned to the O.J. Simpson trial, I wouldn't even know it's raining. Our connection with wildness is inversely proportional to the number of electrical, mechanical, battery-operated and gasoline-driven gadgets we carry with us.

Alpine meadow above the headwaters of the Stikine River

I'm not sure what people from Cleveland or Saskatoon think about as they shuffle along northern highways. They stop only for bad coffee at lodges, at scenic pull-outs where motor homes gather like lemmings, and at RV parks with electrical hook-ups, concrete pads and a few wispy trees. Their trip highlight is a glimpse of a moose's dusty backside disappearing into the shrubbery.

Several years ago a few friends and I drove to Alaska for a kayaking trip. After paddling the Nenana River, we pulled into the parking lot at the Denali National Park visitors' centre. I climbed out of the car and nodded to a man lounging against the side of an Airstream trailer that looked like a fat aluminum cigar.

"Have you tried the Wilderness Simulator?" he asked.

"Pardon me?"

"The Wilderness Simulator!" he shouted, jerking his thumb towards the visitors' centre. "Ask at the front desk."

He wasn't kidding. I followed a crowd into an imposing wooden building. Inside the visitors' centre were photographic displays, stuffed animals, sign-up lists for bus tours and the Wilderness Simulator. It was a small room with video screens, wired for sound. I crowded in with a dozen other road warriors to find out the meaning of wilderness, that mystery beyond the asphalt.

I could only think of two reasons for the Wilderness Simulator. One, an elaborate practical joke. Maybe someone waited with a bucket of ice-cold water mixed with magpie shit to fling on us as we watched the screen. Two, a forward-thinking park manager's brainwave to keep us out of the wilderness, to keep us rolling down the highways where we won't disrupt wildlands.

The B.C. Ministry of Parks is not as prosperous or innovative as the U.S. Parks System. It hasn't installed a Wilderness Simulator for the Stikine. We'll have to endure the real thing.

Our plane swoops west over Spatsizi, a Tahltan First Nation word meaning "red goat," named for mountain goats stained a rusty-red from traversing slopes rich in iron-oxide. I can't see any red goats, but the alpine ridges are reddish gold, tinted by the season's first frosts.

We drop from the clouds and splash down on Tuaton Lake. For Jody and I, this is the beginning of our attempt to paddle the Stikine from its headwaters to the Pacific. Sue Johnson and Arno Springer, friends from Whitehorse, have come with us to canoe the upper river. The pilot cuts the engine and the float plane grounds gently on the gravel shores.

The next morning, Sue and I follow caribou tracks down the beach, through the willows and up into the alpine. We shelter from a bitter south wind in the lee of a ridge. Sue pulls out a compact pair of binoculars, scans the mountains, then peers into a valley below us. A bull moose stands in a swamp, raking its massive antlers against a willow, preparing for the rut. A smaller bull grazes placidly nearby. On our way back to camp, we surprise three young caribou. They skitter towards us, lifting their muzzles. When they catch our scent, they pivot and bolt up a scree slope.

After a couple of days of hiking near the Stikine's headwaters, we load the canoes and paddle downstream. It's a sedate ten-day journey, highlighted by observing wildlife in its natural surroundings. We float past moose, tundra swans and beavers. Ospreys, hawk owls and bald eagles watch our bright boats suspended in the clear water. A porcupine stands with its paws in the stream, nerving itself to plunge in. We hear the howl of a timber wolf from the depths of the forest.

One overcast afternoon a shaft of sunlight breaks through the clouds, lighting a stand of alders, a brilliant yellow-red flame of colour in the forest. Before long we round a corner and see real flames, a forest fire. A few weeks ago the blaze must have straddled the river here, leaping from spruce to spruce in starbursts of exploding sap and burning needles. Today it simmers, dampened by rain and calm weather. Smoke swirls and eddies around our canoes. I pull my sweater over my mouth and nose and breathe through the makeshift filter.

"Looks like more rain," says Arno when we stop to camp somewhere below the confluence of the Spatsizi River. "Let's put up the tarp." On most trips, our tarp is an insurance

Jody perfects his pancake flipping technique

policy, a piece of excess baggage mouldering in the bottom of the boat. On this trip it has rained nearly every day and the tarp is a fixture, the kitchen and dining room of our nomadic camps on the river.

In the night, snow creeps out of the high country and ambushes our camp. When I crawl out of my tent to pee in the darkness, I can feel it falling softly, soggy flakes that melt as they settle on my bare shoulders. By morning, the tent sags under several centimetres of wet snow.

This morning it's Jody's turn to cook breakfast. He gathers a handful of twigs from under a spruce. The twigs break with satisfyingly dry snaps. Jody builds a teepee of driftwood on the fire-pan and torches it with a lighter. He dumps pancake mix into an aluminum pot, adds water and stirs briskly. When the fire burns down to a reddish-orange bed of coals, he settles the cast-aluminum dutch oven on top, rotating the pot to squash the coals into a firm platform.

When the pot is hot he burps oil from a plastic bottle and spoons in batter. "This will be a challenge," he says, "flipping these babies with a fork." He squats at the edge of a spreading circle of melted snow and stares at the pancake, which begins to bubble. He lifts the sides gently. Then, as if to take the pancake by surprise, he jams the fork underneath and lifts vigorously. "Damn," he says as it rips in two, the flipped portion sprawling drunkenly across the other half.

"Don't worry," says Sue, "they'll taste fine."

Jody pokes the pancake. It looks like a char-broiled scrambled egg. "This would be easier if we had a flipper."

"Why don't you flip them in the air?" I suggest.

"Maybe," says Jody, his tone saying that he'd have as much luck willing the pancakes to levitate, "but there's no handle on the dutch oven."

"Use the gloves," says Arno, "grab the side of the pan."

"Okay, okay." He waits until the mangled pancake is cooked and scrapes it into my mug. I drop on a dollop of jam and take a bite. It tastes fine. It tastes like jam. Jody jabs at the next pancake, making sure it's loose, shaking the pan until it slides over the thin layer of oil. "Okay, here goes."

He jerks the dutch oven to chest height. The pancake lifts off and flies gracefully for a moment. Jody is entranced by the sight and he's caught by surprise when the pancake

plummets. He stabs at it with the dutch oven, but the pancake drapes itself over the edge. Batter drips down the outside of the pan and hisses into the fire with tiny puffs of smoke.

"You need more wrist action," says Sue.

"Have another cup of coffee," suggests Arno.

"Just because it looks like I'm not awake," says Jody, "doesn't mean that I am." Jody is highly skilled at many things, but like all of us, he doesn't have complete mastery of his tongue. When we stop laughing, the rest of us try flipping pancakes, with about as much success.

If we were African Bushmen, we'd know that part of our spirit stayed behind at each campsite. Something more than ashes, footprints and canoe tracks in the wet sand. We'd name each camp to ensure that its essence would persist, waiting for our return. The Camp Where the Porcupine Forded the River. The Camp Where Jody Fed Pancakes to the Fire. The Camp Where the Owl Shrieked at the Moon.

We pack up camp while the fire burns to a pile of ash that looks like the down on an owl's breast. We scatter it and smooth the sand behind us. When the boats are packed we slip into the river.

Unless something unforeseen happens, this will be our last night out. Tomorrow we'll round a bend and see the Stewart-Cassiar Highway bridge. We beach our canoes on a gravel bar and Jody and I trot into the forest to look for tent sites. "Too late," he yells. "I've found *the* best spot. It kicks butt."

As dusk falls, a full moon rises above the spruce trees across the river. We sit around waiting for a batch of cinnamon buns to bake. Coals glow on top of the dutch oven and the moon changes from red to orange to yellow as it climbs above the stain of forest fire smoke on the horizon.

We don't talk much. The longer you are out on a trip, the less you need to say. Small talk brings no comfort. Silence is no longer embarrassing. It is never silent anyway. Something is always murmuring, rustling or chattering. Something that tells a story of water flowing to the sea, wind moving through the branches or a red squirrel protesting that we are tenting under her tree.

Cemetary near Telegraph Creek

In the night a harsh scream catches me in the twilight between waking and sleeping. Sue and I wriggle our heads into the night. The sky is tinted by moonlight, only the brighter stars visible. In a scraggly spruce above Jody and Arno's tent, a hooded silhouette blocks the starlight. It swoops on gigantic wings to a branch near us, shrieking mournfully.

It's an owl. I'm sure it's an owl. But it isn't acting like one. Owls perch in trees, hooting, dropping on rodents with silent wings. This creature is wailing like a banshee, flying back and forth between our two tents. It dips so low I can almost hear its talons brushing the fly.

Like many North Americans, I automatically look for order in the world—for behaviour patterns described in *A Field Guide to Western Birds*. The bird can't be frightening us away from a nest. It's too late for nesting season. We're too big for prey. What is it doing? Maybe I shouldn't be seeking a scientific explanation.

The antics of wild creatures were the basis for legends told by First Nations people across the north. A story about another bird, Raven, tells of the liberation of the stars, the moon and the sun from the lodge of a powerful chief who was hoarding them. This legend is told by both Tlingit and Tagish people. The Tagish live in the watersheds just north of the Stikine. Historically, the Tlingit travelled up the Stikine from the coast of Alaska.

In this legend, the daughter of the great chief was bathing near a stream. Raven, the trickster, turned himself into a microscopic spruce needle that fell into a handful of water that the young woman was drinking. Once inside her body, he turned himself into a baby, a baby that the great chief came to love after its birth.

Children are able to twist their grandparents around their little fingers, and this was no exception. The chief allowed Raven-baby to play with the moon and stars, and the trickster deliberately let them escape, up through the smoke hole in the lodge and into the heavens. The baby turned himself back into Raven and fled with the sun, soot from the smoke-hole blackening his feathers during his escape. Light was brought to the world.

In the Yukon, Raven is still a bringer of light. The streetlights in Whitehorse are activated by darkness,

illuminating the roads after the sun sinks over the horizon. On bitterly cold winter days, Raven huddles over a streetlight, spreading its dark wings like a cloak. In the shadow of the black feathers, the lamp turns on, bringing light, but more importantly for Raven, warmth that seeps up through the metal casing.

Raven's voice, especially on a minus forty degree day, carries a disturbing intelligence. I could believe a legend about a raven. And what about the bird screaming outside our tent on the Stikine? It deserves a story. The owl, if that is what it is, shrieks in funereal tones, swoops low over our tent and finally vanishes in the forest.

But in the morning, we'll hear trucks and motor homes rattling down the highway even before we see the bridge. We'll re-enter the 1990s. Tomorrow night the reflections in the windows will wash out the night sky. We'll turn up the stereo to drown the silence. Televisions will hypnotize us with their lurid stare. We'll read newspapers, listen to the radio, find out what's been going on in the world.

I'll tell my family about the owl, but they'll be too absorbed by the hustle of the world to pay much attention. How can an oddly behaving owl compete with Nirvana or REM? With the CBC News on the Hour? With *Rolling Stone Magazine* or the *Globe and Mail*? I hope at least my memories survive the sensory glare.

Waterfall at the headwaters of the Stikine

(above) Tahltan children explore Jody's kayak at Telegraph Creek

THE PUT-IN

"The spare is flat too," says Jody glumly, crawling out from under the truck.

We're stuck 50 kilometres out from Dease Lake. We had planned to have a relaxing evening at the put-in for the Grand Canyon of the Stikine. Now the front passenger-side tire is flat and so is the spare and we haven't passed another vehicle since we left Telegraph Creek.

"I should have checked the spare before we left Whitehorse," says Jody, kicking the flat tire disgustedly.

"Forget it. It's exactly the kind of thing I'd do."

"What a drag! Who is going to be driving down the Telegraph Creek Road on a Labour Day weekend Saturday night?"

I grab the jack. "Let's whip this tire off. If anyone comes, I'll hitchhike into Dease Lake with it."

Jody chips several thousand kilometres worth of petrified mud from the axle while I loosen the lug nuts. We hoist the truck on the ancient jack and slide off the wheel. I prop it against the side of the truck. Then I load a day-pack with a sleeping bag and toothbrush in case I can't get the tire fixed tonight.

I pace on the road until I get bored, then grab a book from my pack and crawl up on the hood. Jody pulls out a pair of grocery bags and starts waterproofing his trip food. Ninety minutes later, I hear approaching traffic. I walk out on the road and wave my arms. A low-slung Mercury skids to a halt. Dust settles over Jody's food bags. The driver rolls down his window. A pair of women sit beside him. The back seat is brimming with kids.

"Thanks for stopping," I say. "I need to get into Dease Lake to get this flat fixed."

The driver stares at me for a moment then swivels his head like an owl and stares at the back seat. "I suppose we can find room."

I shove the flat tire into the trunk and elbow myself some space in the back seat beside three young children. Each kid clutches an Archie comic book. "That was nice of you to pick me up," I say brightly. "There's not much traffic on this road. You folks live around here?"

The driver's eyes glance in my direction morosely, "No."

"Oh! I guess you're on holiday, eh?

"No."

"Oh, that right? So, where are you from, anyway?"

"Watson."

With my store of small talk depleted I sit back and stare out the window. The kids poke each other and giggle, but they don't talk either. Forty-five minutes later we rattle into Dease Lake. I retrieve the tire and wave as the Mercury heads north up the Stewart-Cassiar Highway.

It's Saturday night in Dease Lake and the pick-ups are cruising restlessly. Up to the junction of the Telegraph Creek Road, turning, spinning wheels between the store and a dusty softball diamond. And back again, like leaves swirling in an eddy. I roll the tire towards the Shell sign down the road.

"Sorry man," says the gas jockey when I carry in the tire. "The guy who fixes flats has gone home for the day. I'll try calling him." He dials, but there is no answer. "Look, it's Saturday night. He'll be out driving around. He has a green crew cab, a Dodge. Flag him down if you see him. Or you can try the Esso station down the highway, but I think it's closed."

I run south on the highway, past the café where half a dozen trucks are idling. No green Dodge. Past the RCMP station and a new restaurant that looks like it belongs at the off-ramp of a freeway. At the Esso station the garage is covered by a giant orange tarp and a "closed" sign. I'm about to go looking for the green Dodge when I notice a mobile home behind the garage. The windows flicker with the unearthly blue glow of a television. I walk over and pound on the door.

"Yeah?"

I open the door, walk into a hallway and peer into the living room. A young man with oily black hair is stretched out on a couch watching a baseball game. I can tell he's a mechanic by the dark smears of grease across his t-shirt. In this light, it's hard to tell if it's a blotch of oil or a moustache on his upper lip.

"Excuse me, but I've got a flat tire outside. Our truck is stranded up the Telegraph Creek Road."

"Can't do it." He stares at the men standing around on bright green astroturf. "You a Blue Jays fan? The Jays are

Autumn colours in the boreal forest

behind 3-2 in the bottom of the fifth. They've got a man on third, but there's two out."

"Look, I know it's Saturday night, but we're stuck. I'm willing to pay extra if you could fix it." I wait for an answer, looking at the screen. Paul Molitor steps out of the batter's box, spits and stares at the third base coach. He takes a high slider. Finally he strikes out, looking at a fast ball on the outside corner.

"Shit!" says the mechanic, stabbing at the screen with the remote control. "Okay, where's your tire?"

Half an hour later I'm trotting down the road, rolling the tire in front of me, slapping it with a little topspin to keep it moving. It doesn't take long to reach the outskirts of town. I plunk the tire in the dirt as the last light fades from the sky.

The sparse traffic is local, mostly trucks on the outside periphery of their circuits, satellites held in by the gravitational pull of downtown Dease Lake. I squat down, grab a handful of rocks and toss them desultorily at a telephone pole. When I hit the pole I take a step backward and when I miss, a step forward. Hitchhiker's recreational pursuits, memories from the '60s, when I rode my thumb across Canada.

Then a single headlight turns from a side road and I stick out my thumb. A pick-up chugs down the road and stops beside me. "Where you headed with that tire?" asks a young voice in a large, adult body.

"Forty or fifty kilometres down the road towards Telegraph Creek."

"Heck, I can give you a ride out there." I fling the tire and my day pack into the back and jump in the cab. "My name's Mark. I think I better stop at Mom and Dan's to get our spare tire. It wouldn't be too cool to join you out there with a flat." He detours to a house behind the Dease Lake airstrip, throws a spare in the back and bounces back to the Telegraph Creek Road.

"How long have you lived in Dease Lake?" I ask.

"I'm not from here, at least not for the last few years." Mark peers out of a windshield that is pocked with scars from flying rocks. "I've been down in Prince George with my father. I've only been back up here since June. Most of the kids here don't like me, probably because I'm from the city. One guy always wants to fight me, but I'm just not a fighter. That's the worst thing on the planet, always wondering when he'll come over and start pushing me around."

I dredge similar memories from 25 years ago (can it really be a quarter of a century?) and agree with Mark. We sink into silence. He is no doubt thinking about bullies. I'm thinking about a quarter of a century.

"What kind of vehicle you got out there?"

"It's a Toyota," I answer. "Jody's old Toyota truck."

"I'm a Chevy guy myself." Mark thumps the steering wheel. "This Ford is Dan's, he's my mom's boyfriend. He's the best mechanic at Yellowhead Road and Bridge. I can't figure out why he drives a Ford. Yeah, I'm into Chevys." He turns and looks at me. "What are you guys doing here?"

"Well, we were just coming back from Telegraph Creek."

"I'm related to just about everybody in Telegraph Creek."

"Are you from the Tahltan First Nation?"

"Yeah," he says, nodding his head. "I'm also related to everybody in Dease Lake. I'm related to *just* about everyone in Iskut. Heck, I've got relatives in Seattle, in Manitoba and even in Switzerland."

"That doesn't surprise me," I say. "I've heard that the Tahltans have always been travellers, moving here from the north and trading with the Tlingits down at the mouth of the Stikine."

"I wouldn't know about that. Our teachers never told us anything about the Tahltans. The only native culture they taught in school was junk about the Haidas and totem poles."

"Have things changed now? Are the kids learning about their own culture?"

"Naw. Not unless they've changed the textbooks since I was here a couple of years ago, but I doubt it."

Dan's Ford rattles down the road, its single headlight shining weakly. I can see the dusty edge of the spruce forest that borders the twisting road. Behind that is darkness, mile after mile of darkness, stretching hundreds of kilometres north to the Alaska Highway.

"I'm a careful driver," says Mark, staring through the splintered glass. "Eighty kilometres on the flats and slower on the curves. Not like my aunt, now she drives *fast*. No shit. She has only one speed. Fast."

Mark talks about driving the road to Telegraph Creek, about his aunt, about a friend of his who drove off the road in a Suburban four-wheel drive station-wagon. I tune out for

Sunset through the towering walls of the Grand Canyon of the Stikine

a moment and start daydreaming about the Grand Canyon. Suddenly I know that we are actually going to begin paddling tomorrow. We've passed the point of no return.

I spoke to two Stikine veterans before we left Whitehorse, Rob Lesser and Doug Ammons. Rob was the first kayaker to dream that the canyon could be paddled. These are two of the most experienced wildwater paddlers in the world. They made it clear that the Stikine is a serious river. A river to be approached warily, with your ego tucked firmly away. Doug gave me a piece of advice. "Be paranoid." Easy advice to follow.

Fear is a part of any wilderness adventure. It follows behind you, usually an unobtrusive companion, hiding from the light like a shadow. But sometimes, when you're headed for a place as wild as the Stikine, you drag your fear like a ball and chain.

Suddenly my heart pounds faster. What am I doing? Beads of sweat form on my forehead. The best paddlers in the world are intimidated by the Grand Canyon of the Stikine! What am I doing here? Then I hear Mark say that his friend in the Suburban was lucky, she ran over 20 small alders but only dented her fender. My wave of panic recedes, like a tsunami churning back out to sea, leaving a vague, dreamy recollection of fear, and fingertips that tingle.

"You think *I'm* into Chevys," says Mark, "I've got this one friend—a crazy French guy. Name's Ben, Ben Gay. He's *really* into Chevys. He says Fords suck, big time. He says Dodges have *no* power. He drives like an idiot, into swamps or through creeks…it doesn't matter to Ben. One time he tried to cross this creek and the water was deeper than he thought. The water came right up to the door and I said, 'Be-en, the water is coming into the cab.' He says, 'So what! We're in a Chevy, right?' And he guns it right up the bank."

Mark tells me about Dease Lake on a Saturday night, about the parties hidden within the orbits of the pick-ups. He talks about drinking, about drugs. "My dad thinks I use drugs because I hang around with people who do. But I don't. He lets me drink, in fact he gives me tea and rum. I don't drink beer. It's gotta be the *worst* liquid on this planet. It tastes like horse piss."

"What were you doing in Telegraph Creek?" he asks.

"We dropped some gear off. Now we're headed to kayak down the Stikine."

"Man!" says Mark. "You wouldn't get me in a kayak. I

have a friend who wanted me to go bungy jumping, but there was no *way* I'd do it. Then, when we took a trip to Victoria, he wanted me to jump off a pier into the ocean. There's no way I'd do that either. There are jellyfish and all kinds of gross things in salt water. There's no *way* I'd jump in there."

We round the corner and see the truck. Jody is sleeping, resigned to spending the night. "Hey Jode," I shake his tent. "Wake up. We're heading for the river."

While Jody and I change the tire, Mark gives us tire repair tips. "Hey," he says. "Dan keeps a pump in the back of the truck! It runs off a twelve volt battery. We could fill up that spare…maybe it just has a slow leak."

Mark hooks the pump up to Jody's battery. The pump whirrs and the tire gradually swells. He seems shy all of a sudden, now that he's out of Dan's truck, now that Jody and I are bustling around, our lives back in control. When we're all packed up, I give Mark ten dollars for gas, shake his hand and thank him.

"I like helping people," he says.

We follow Mark back into Dease Lake, in case one of us gets another flat. The road seems less lonely now that we are in convoy. Even though I'm separated from Mark by a couple of metal shells, I can still hear him talking about his life in this remote northern town.

"You know," Jody says, "When I was flaked out in the tent, it seemed like that flat tire was a test of our determination to get on the river." He grins at me. "I guess we passed the test."

At Dease Lake Mark stops along the side of the road and Jody pulls up alongside. I roll down my window, reach over and shake his hand again. "You saved our asses," I say. He smiles, puts the Ford in gear and jostles down the road towards his house.

We turn south on the Stewart-Cassiar Highway. "That Mark is a neat kid," I say. I babble to Jody about the things he told me—his fears, his friends, his taste in automobiles. "It's a drag how we insulate ourselves from people with different backgrounds. We surround ourselves with friends who have similar interests, similar feelings about life. I don't have a single friend who is a Chevy guy like Mark."

It suddenly seems tragic that I'll likely never see Mark again.

Jody loads his kayak at the put-in

THE STIKINE TOAD-FROG

There's a strip of sky, but no sunshine touches the depths of the Grand Canyon of the Stikine. Sculptured bedrock walls rise vertically from the river. Above them, pastel-tinted sedimentary cliffs float in the clouds like a mirage. Downstream, the river is swallowed by dark granite.

From river level, the Grand Canyon is all-encompassing. Some god at the dawn of time must have drawn a blade across the land, slicing through layers of conglomerates and sandstones, scoring deep into the underlying bedrock. The river itself is that god, but it began cutting into the Stikine Plateau only a few hundred thousand years ago. The canyon is a youngster in geologic time.

In the calm between rapids the river is dark and oily looking. A small shape bobs near a vertical bedrock wall. A whirlpool tugs at it, sucks it under and pops it to the surface downstream. I paddle over to investigate.

"Look at this," I yell to Jody. "A toad!" Amphibians are uncommon in the north and the Stikine Canyon is a bizarre place to find one. "Here buddy, you'll be safer inside my kayak." I grab the toad, pop my spray deck and tuck it inside.

The throaty roar of whitewater echoes around the corner and my pulse accelerates. The rapids are overpowering: steep drops, intimidating holes, huge waves, exploding turbulence. My pre-trip jitters would have been much worse if I had known the reality of the Stikine.

"This must be 'The Wall,'" says Jody.

I remember what Doug Ammons had written about "The Wall." "Big lead-in slams into the wall…make sure you can get centre-left for the bottom half. Death on river right."

We pull in and wedge our kayaks on a granite reef jutting into the river. To scout the rapid we traverse along water-polished, satin smooth walls. I curl my fingers over hand-holds or jam them into cracks before moving my feet. A slip would mean drowning. We can't see much, just the horizon line where the river plunges into an old rock slide. There is no way to portage.

"What do you think?"

"I'm going to be *there*," Jody answers, pointing to a gap between a pair of huge boulders.

I'd like to linger and stare at the rapid. There is some comfort in fantasizing that there are options. Then black spots of moisture appear on the granite. Raindrops. "Let's just do it," I say, "before the rock gets too slippery to climb back to our kayaks."

Back at my boat, the toad is squatting on the bow deck like a lumpy hood ornament. It sits motionless, as if waiting for me. I slip my fingers under its belly. "This is better than trying to swim," I murmur, shoving it back into the gloomy interior of my kayak.

Jody goes first. The powerful current whisks him out of sight. The toad and I are on our own. When I paddle into the current I feel tiny toes through my long underwear, sharp toes scratching and scrabbling. A damp blob clambers onto my ankle. I float into the rapid, not paddling aggressively enough. My bow stalls in a curling wave and I cartwheel in slow motion.

I've flipped at least a dozen times in the canyon so far. My roll has been reliable but this time I feel disoriented. The boat responds sluggishly, as if I'm mired in maple syrup. I flop under the surface and try again. And again. I switch sides, sweep my paddle, flip my hips…and sink. My hand twitches to pull off my spray deck, the first step in bailing out of a kayak, but swimming is unthinkable. I grip my paddle and set up again. I'm surprised to emerge into daylight.

"Paddle!" shouts Jody from an eddy. "Go for it."

In what seems like a blind stroke of fortune, my kayak is perfectly positioned above the gap we'd pointed to from shore. I have time for three quick strokes and a couple of breaths before the bottom drops out of the rapid and I flip again. There is no point trying to roll in a liquid hurricane, so I hang on.

The silty water suddenly turns darker. I'm washing into an undercut wall. I try to roll, but my paddle grinds against vertical rock. Then I'm up, floating in calm water beside the cliff, gulping sweet air. I look upstream. The bright blue bottom of Jody's boat looks tiny in the cascade. He rolls up and paddles over.

"Don't do that again, Ken." He shakes his head.

"I wonder how the toad is? That was worse than Mr. Toad's

Jody running a rapid in the Grand Canyon

wild ride in the *Wind in the Willows*." Joking is better than thinking about the immediate future.

It is too turbulent to check on the toad, so we paddle downstream. After several kilometres the granite walls back away from the river temporarily, replaced by desert-like sandstone cliffs. Kayakers named this section of the Grand Canyon the "Garden of the Gods." We drag our kayaks onto the rocks. The toad squats like Buddha on the bottom of my boat.

"It looks okay," says Jody.

I cup the toad between my hands and carry it through a field of loose boulders. I place it beneath a few scraggly alders and return to the river. We camp just downstream, at the only sandy beach in the heart of the Grand Canyon.

The night before we had slept at "Site Zed," a motley outpost of prefab shacks perched on a shelf deep in the canyon. Site Zed was B.C. Hydro's choice for the largest of their fantasy dams—a 75-storey-high giant that would have flooded the Grand Canyon and backed up the river for 80 kilometres. The engineers chose an impressive spot with 400 metre walls rising straight up from the river. One cliff reminded me of a dark, brooding version of Yosemite's El Capitan.

From an engineer's point of view, this deep canyon is a gigantic trough, a place to store millions of cubic metres of water. It's the same perspective on the natural world that sees a tree in terms of board-feet, or a forest as vertical lumber storage.

There are parallels between the Glen Canyon Dam on the Colorado River and what may yet happen to the Grand Canyon of the Stikine. Edward Abbey floated through Glen Canyon just before the dam was completed in 1963. Abbey described his feelings in his book *Desert Solitaire*:

"To grasp the nature of the crime that was committed, imagine the Taj Mahal or Chartres Cathedral buried in mud until only the spires remain visible. With this difference: those man-made celebrations of human aspiration could conceivably be reconstructed while Glen Canyon was a living thing, irreplaceable, which can never be recovered through any human agency."

In the 1970s, B.C. Hydro opened the public purse to the

tune of 50 million dollars for its scheme to turn the Grand Canyon into Lake Stikine. Helicopters buzzed in and out of the canyon while engineers pored over blueprints. Miners blasted shafts into living rock. Only B.C. Hydro employees heard the explosions. And mountain goats. And maybe a stray toad. But they don't count. They don't have a financial stake. The Grand Canyon is just their home.

In the '80s, environmental protests, staggering proposed construction costs, and reduced energy demand halted the project. The developers at B.C. Hydro are coy about their future plans for damming the Stikine—like good politicians they've learned to postpone controversy. I'm sure they are poised to pull out the blueprints and dust off the explosives when economic conditions are favourable.

"The Grand Canyon is not identified in our plans for the next decade," a Hydro spokesperson told me in 1994. "The Stikine is an available resource, but new projects in undeveloped watersheds are a low priority." I asked why B.C. Hydro had spent $500,000 in 1989 to install satellite sensing devices. After a stony silence he said that this sort of outlay "is routine."

Even if I wasn't told outright lies, I didn't hear the truth.

As world petroleum reserves shrink, electricity demand will surely magnify. Hydro Quebec, the same outfit that brought us the Great Whale Project, is investing tens of millions of dollars in electric car battery research. Developers are planning for recharging stations every 50 kilometres along busy highways. Motorists in Los Angeles and Phoenix may soon look north for electricity to charge up their batteries.

What will happen if they build a dam at Site Zed? You'll be able to load a jet-boat onto a trailer and drive to Lake Stikine. Your engine's roar will echo from mud-stained walls where mountain goats used to climb. Water-skiers rejoice! This will be your chance to cut figure-8s through the natural world's version of the Sistine Chapel. Beer cans, motor oil and cigarette butts will float in the Grand Canyon of the Stikine, just as they do in Glen Canyon.

Dams don't just drown upstream lands. Unusual turbulence, temperature changes and oxygen deficient releases from Lake Stikine will affect fish far below the face

B.C. Hydro's Site Zed

of the dam itself. The rich salmon spawning grounds in the lower reaches of the canyon will be threatened.

And what about later, when the salmon stocks are diminished and the goats are long gone? After the heavy silt load of the Stikine inevitably fills in the dam? Don Moore, a B.C. Hydro geologist summed it up succinctly for *Harrowsmith Magazine*: "Well, you glaze it over with topsoil and you have the best farmland in the north…with one hell of a waterfall at the end."

I have a better idea. Let's dam Vancouver. The office towers near the B.C. Hydro building soar in the sky like canyon walls. Let Hydro's engineers go wild. Let them fill in the spaces along the street with more high-rises until their glittering facades form solid walls. Let them pile layer after layer of concrete and steel across the bottom of the street. Vancouver's winter monsoons will fill the dam. Hydro executives can indulge in an electrical orgy in their own front yard, and leave the Stikine's goats alone.

Grey-suited or spike-heeled creatures may experience some temporary inconvenience and displacement, but don't worry. They are not an endangered species.

The evening sun is golden on the walls of the Garden of the Gods but I can barely keep my eyes open. For the past few nights I've fallen asleep as if drugged, but woken up after four or five hours, my brain working overtime.

I've heard about downpours that soak the unstable cliffs and loosen boulders that crash into the river, about rains that cause dramatic floods within the Stikine's narrow rock corridor. I lay awake, fretting that a wall of clouds will creep in from the Pacific, until another bright dawn dispels at least that worry.

Jody paddles magnificently during our last day of challenging whitewater. I paddle to survive. I'm tired and my adrenaline reserves are sucked dry. I've been extended to the limit of my abilities for the past three days. Now I just want to get out of here alive.

A boom and a series of thuds echo across the river as a boulder the size of a bowling ball plummets into the water. Smaller rocks clatter in its wake and ribbons of dust writhe along the cliffs. A shaggy nanny goat and her kid stand on a ledge, peering down at our kayaks, dots of colour on the slate-

grey water. Tiny trees on the canyon rim sway in the wind. At water level, the air is unnaturally still.

We pull over at a rapid where the Stikine's roar echoes from the cliffs like the growl of a prehistoric beast. The river drops over a ledge into a hideous hole. We've run harder rapids, but today my instinct is to look for a portage route. I want to save my dwindling energy for rapids I *have* to run. To portage, though, I'll have to stop in a micro-eddy across the river. Missing the eddy will mean slamming into a jumble of boulders.

"I'll paddle down," says Jody calmly. "Then I'll climb back up and grab your boat in the eddy." And he does.

We've set a pattern, a routine for the day. Jody looks for the best line in ridiculously violent rapids. I search for portage routes. There's a role-reversal in our relationship. Not that long ago Jody looked to me for guidance during river trips. Now he is the calm one, with a core of reserve strength that steadies my quivering nerves.

Jody gets creamed in a scary rapid called "The Scissors," rolls up nonchalantly and clambers back to help me carry my boat. "The Hole That Ate Chicago" is impossible to portage, but at least my roll is working again when I find myself upside-down. Our world is a blur of flying spray and solid granite.

We both portage a rapid that looks unrunnable. I tie throw lines to the kayaks and belay the rope while Jody guides them down a boulder garden. We have to jump between a pair of damp rocks with the river slamming beneath us. I imagine the consequences of slipping—falling ten feet onto slick rocks, wedged helplessly in the current with a broken ankle and little chance of rescue. Jody leaps across easily. Each minute of procrastination makes the jump more intimidating, but I have no other choice.

In the late afternoon we reach the "Room of Doom," an hourglass-shaped crucible at the end of the hardest whitewater. The river slips out of the grotto through a two-metre-wide slot. Jody paddles through casually, but when I try, my bow catches on a protruding bedrock knob. I flip sideways, broach in the narrows and hang upside-down for a couple of heartbeats. Eventually the current uncorks me and I roll up in a broad pool.

Jody laughs at my undignified exit. It's a reminder that

Mountain goat perched above the Stikine

we have not "conquered" the Stikine. There are powerful forces at work in this canyon. Somehow we've been allowed to pass through safely.

We camp once more and the next morning float through a volcanic wonderland. Eruptions from nearby Mount Edziza have periodically flooded the lower Grand Canyon with molten basalt. We pass fire-tempered geometric columns in ebony, red and ochre. Sunburst-coloured oxides look as if they are still too hot to touch after passing through the liquid fire of the earth's core.

Mount Edziza's eruptions shaped more than the landscape, they also influenced the culture of the indigenous Tahltan people. The Tahltans collected obsidian—a hard, glassy rock formed when lava cools rapidly—and crafted it into razor-sharp knives and arrowheads. Obsidian was an important trade item, and the Tahltans bartered it with the Kaska and Sekani in the interior and with the Tlingits on the coast. Through this trading network, obsidian from Mount Edziza spread to southeast Alaska, Alberta, and as far south as Oregon.

Jody and I stop for lunch at the confluence of the Tahltan River, a rich salmon spawning ground and a sacred place for the Tahltan people. Across the river is a basalt monolith inset with patches of gold and red that look like the outstretched wings of a giant bird. For centuries, the Tlingits paddled upstream to this spot in their great seafaring canoes. They picked berries, hunted, dried salmon and traded with the Tahltans. We squirm back into our kayaks for the last time and float through the relatively placid lower reaches of the canyon.

Telegraph Creek, the only town on the banks of the Stikine, is a ramshackle collection of Victorian homes and broad-axed log cabins. The townsite, now home to about three hundred people, was at the head of navigation for riverboats steaming up the Stikine during gold rushes in the late 1800s. A couple of aluminum riverboats tug gently at their tethers.

I'm drained, strung out on too much adrenaline and too little sleep. My stomach muscles are tender and my left leg bruised. Jody's hands are blistered with rope-burn from a pair of arduous portages above Site Zed. His long underwear is shredded from abrasive rock, his exposed skin swollen from blackfly bites.

We walk up a dirt road looking for a telephone. A row of cottonwoods with yellowing leaves lines the embankment,

shading a wooden riverboat riding a pair of sawhorses. Two men chat beside an idling pick-up. They smile and nod at us, despite our tangled hair and ragged long underwear. We walk into a building nearly 100 years old, the Stikine RiverSong General Store and Cafe. The phone is beside the window overlooking the river, kitty-corner from shelves holding an eclectic range of goods: bananas to baseball hats, motor oil to mozzarella.

I punch in my home number and talk to Wendy. I tell her that I missed her and Malcolm. I tell her that staring death in the face for four days has made me realize what is *really* important. I'm hoping to convince her to drive 700 bumpy kilometres so I can see them for a few days. After that, I'm paddling solo down to the Pacific, to take more photographs for an article in *Canadian Geographic*.

Jody, who is heading south to go to school in Vancouver, hitches a ride into Dease Lake with the local Catholic priest. It's an abrupt good-bye. One moment we're sharing the most intense outdoor experience of our lives, then he's gone. Out on the Telegraph Creek Road, all that remains is a head full of memories.

The next morning I plunk my day pack beside the road to hitchhike into Dease Lake to meet Wendy and Malcolm. A few blackflies buzz lazily around my head. In front of the school, a group of high school students throw a football back and forth. Around back, a dozen horses stand in the adventure playground, swishing their tails. A peregrine falcon swoops over the school and glides towards the river.

After a couple of hours a brown truck bounces around the corner and skids to a stop. There's an eagle painted on the hood, an eagle with wings outstretched, prepared for flight. The driver, a solidly-built young Tahltan man, stares at me suspiciously and flings open the back of the canopy.

"If you want a ride," he says, "everything has to go in the back, including your jacket."

"Are you serious?"

"I haven't picked up a hitchhiker in years, not since a white guy pulled a knife on me. I don't know why I stopped

Jody squeezes through the "Tanzilla Slot"

for you. *Everything* has to go in the back."

I chuck my pack beside a pile of spare tires and a dented toolbox. Everything is layered with a film of dust. I take off my jacket and wedge it under the pack. A man slouched in the front seat opens the passenger door and I squeeze into the back of the king cab. A toddler with enormous brown eyes stares at me shyly from under a pile of blankets.

"I'm Gilbert," says the driver. He gestures to his companion. "This is Albert."

Gilbert lets out the clutch and we lurch forward. He reaches over and fiddles with the stereo. A Randy Travis song booms out. The boy looks at me solemnly and holds up a ragged stuffed animal that might be a bear, or a lion. He speaks to me with a voice too soft to hear. I lean towards him, but the flow of words trickles from his lips and melts into the throbbing country rhythm.

With one hand on the steering wheel Gilbert leans on the accelerator and we rocket towards Dease Lake. We meet an oncoming oil truck. Each vehicle is like a comet trailing a plume of dust much larger than itself. Gilbert drives through the dust-cloud without hitting the brakes. There is no way he can see anything, he must be steering by instinct.

He leans over and looks at me, "You been working in Telegraph Creek?"

"No, a friend and I just kayaked the Stikine."

"You put in at the Tahltan?"

"No, we did the whole Grand Canyon. We started at the Stewart-Cassiar Highway."

He looks surprised. He says that the Stikine is some wild river, that a few years ago, a pair of kayakers who put in at the Tahltan ended up face down, entangled in his friend's salmon net. "The spirits of our ancestors must have watched you from the canyon rim," he says. "What do you think of our country?"

My imagination is still at river level, staring up at towering walls, awed by thundering rapids. I have no trouble talking about how the land impressed me. Gilbert swivels his head and stares at me, his dark eyes deep as the canyon itself. "If you feel that way," he says, "are you going to help us fight B.C. Hydro's dam project?"

I nod my head, but I don't know what to say. As a white man of European descent I feel partly responsible for our callous indifference to wildlands. Places like the Grand

Canyon must be left alone. Not because it has splendid recreational value. It doesn't. Not because it has rich tourism potential. It doesn't. It must be protected simply because it is. Ask the goats. Ask the Tahltans.

I have trouble finding coherent words, so I tell him about my environmental work. I talk about the lessons that we learned during the Tatshenshini-Alsek campaign. "What happened during the 1970s with the Tahltans and B.C. Hydro?" I ask. I'd heard stories of gunfire, damaged helicopters and burning fuel dumps. Gilbert isn't into reminiscing though, he wants to talk about the future.

"There's a new generation of warriors here. If B.C. Hydro comes back *we'll* be the ones to get out the dynamite this time." He throws his arm out the window. "This is our land. We've hunted in this valley for centuries. If they drive away the moose, what will we eat? This isn't cattle country. Tahltans aren't beef eaters."

"The land around the rim of the canyon is sacred to us," he says. "It is our home." His words echo what other aboriginal people have told me, that they have no word for "wilderness." Their intimate relationship with the land makes it not a wild place, but a home-place.

After a while I tell them about the toad I met in the canyon. While I'm talking the boy curls up on the seat and falls asleep. Gilbert leans back, hooks a blanket with strong fingers and gently drapes it over him.

"You know," Gilbert says in a matter-of-fact voice, "before whites brought smallpox into this country, there was a frog clan in the Tahltan Nation. That frog you carried in your kayak was one of our ancestors. It was there to guide you safely through the canyon so you could help us fight B.C. Hydro. Now I know why I stopped to pick you up back at Telegraph."

I've always been a skeptic about the supernatural. I wonder whether he is joking, but he looks and sounds serious. Later I find out that Tahltan tradition includes a belief in sorcery and animal spirits.

Guidance from a frog? Maybe I should pay more attention to the small creatures on earth. Maybe Gilbert is right. The magic of the Stikine is too powerful to take lightly.

First Nation petroglyph beside the Great River

RIVERBOATS ON THE STIKINE

Thick grey clouds spill over the granite spires of the Coast Mountains. A squall races up the lower Stikine, whipping up standing waves and blowing spray in my face. Ahead I see an abandoned homestead behind a barrier of huge cottonwoods. I drag my sea kayak up a silty beach covered with wolf and grizzly tracks. A trail through the woods leads to a log house.

The outside woodwork is rough, but the door handles have been carved with painstaking care. Yellow gingham curtains hang in the kitchen windows. I walk into a child's bedroom, push aside a stuffed tiger and sit on a rudimentary bunk bed. I leaf through old books in a homemade wooden bookcase. I find a copy of *Practical Arithmetics*. Someone has crossed out the words "Property of the town of Morrill, 1937," and printed "Alexander" in neat block letters.

Who built this cabin? Back-to-the-land hippies during the sixties? Religious fundamentalists hiding from the evils of the modern world? I set up my stove on the kitchen table. While pasta is simmering I find a hand-made broom, sweep mouse shit off a bed frame, and lay out my sleeping bag.

The clouds vanish overnight. Frost sparkles in the cottonwoods. Steam rises from the river. I hear the falsetto shriek of a bald eagle and the chatter of boreal chickadees. I pick a mug-full of strawberries from an overgrown garden and add it to my granola.

As I paddle towards the coast, the dry hillsides in the highlands change to old-growth rain forest. Spruce and hemlock trees droop under a thick layer of moss. The bright whites and blues of glaciers flowing down from the mountains contrast sharply with the dark forest green.

Everywhere there is life. In the water, coho salmon splash and leap, pursued by harbour seals. On land, moose crash through the underbrush and bears chew spawned-out salmon. In the air, eagles flap lazily and Vs of Canada geese migrate southwards. There are people too. I pass several salmon fishing outposts: a family business, a Tahltan camp and a co-operative complete with bunkhouses, half-a-dozen aluminum launches and a packing plant.

Six days after leaving Telegraph Creek, I paddle into Alaska.

There are no sentries at the border, my entry into the U.S. just another paddle stroke in the driving rain. From the middle of the broad Stikine, the mountainsides appear as dark lines in the grey mist. A jet boat zooms upstream. A red-shirted man holds up a rifle in what I hope is a friendly wave.

I hear a whine that becomes a roar as a huge hovercraft flies downriver. It looks like an apparition with its flashing lights and cushion of spray. The hover-freighter transports gold ore from Cominco's mine on the Iskut River down to Wrangell. People who fish upstream complain that its wake erodes the riverbanks and chokes prime fishing eddies with debris. A Cominco spokesperson told me that the hovercraft was "an environmentally friendly alternative to a road." Smart tactics—compare something bad with something worse.

The Stikine delta is an intricate system of sloughs, islands and tidal flats created from the rich cargo of silt and rotting salmon carried down from the interior. The estuary is a major resting spot along the Pacific flyway. Half a million migratory birds stop here each year, including sandhill cranes, snow geese and trumpeter swans. I'd like to explore, but I have a northbound ferry to catch in Wrangell.

Wrangell has sprung up on a peninsula surrounded by a rich natural world: the fertile rainforest, the living sea, the Great River. There is a Wild West feel to the town. Every driveway has a truck. Every truck has a gun rack. Bumper stickers read "Loggers are an Endangered Species Too" and "Eat moose—12,000 wolves can't be wrong." I have an uneasy feeling in town. Maybe I've just been on the river too long, but Wrangell, like many small, resource-based towns, seems to live off the land without paying its respects to mother earth.

I haul my sea kayak to the ferry terminal. I have a few hours to kill, so I telephone Dan Gross. I've heard he is the last surviving pilot of the riverboats that used to chug up the lower Stikine. He invites me over for a cup of coffee.

He stands at the top of a rickety set of stairs. He's a big man wearing jeans and a neatly pressed shirt. It is hard to tell his age, over 70 for sure. He is a little flabby now, but I can see he was once solid muscle. He looks at my beard and tangled hair suspiciously, then ushers me inside and pours me a cup of coffee.

Volcanic rock walls in the Grand Canyon

He talks stiffly at first, answering questions with monosyllables. Getting him to talk is like picking away at a plugged drain. It takes a while to break through the reserve, but eventually his memories gush out.

"I was 12 when Sid Barrington hired me as a deckhand," he says. "My main job was to measure the river's depth with a pole so the boat could nose upriver without running aground. Sid was the best riverboat captain around. Crabby though, he was gruff as a goat."

"Men worked in those days." He stares at me as if wondering whether I'd ever done a real day's work. "Those were rough and rowdy times. You worked so hard you'd lose your marbles. When you weren't working, you drank hard. In 1938, I was the pilot on the *Hazel B*. During World War II we hauled D-8 cats and every blooming thing they needed to build the military airport at Watson Lake."

"The Stikine can be a treacherous river. It took four or five days to get to Telegraph Creek. At Snaggy Bend, you really had to have your marbles in your head. There was high water, low water, stumps, logs—you name it. Snaggy Bend was a dirty rotten place to come down. And icebergs! When I was a boy, the Great Glacier came right down to the river, calving bergs straight into the water."

"Riverboats were my life." He sounds sad, yearning for his lost youth. "If it wasn't for the fact that most people moved out of Telegraph Creek, I'd still be on the river."

"Has the Stikine changed much over the years?"

"The traffic is worse. The whole damn town roars upriver in their jet boats. They call it moose hunting, but mostly they just get drunk and shoot off automatic rifles. Out at my cabin near the mouth of the river you could get shot while sitting in the outhouse. The other thing is the wildlife. You don't see many animals on the Stikine anymore. Too many people."

He asks about my trip on the river. He stands up and stares out the window while I'm talking. It is still raining and a gust of wind rattles the window panes. He seems more relaxed, as if acknowledging a bond between us since we've travelled the same river.

"I guess I should head back. Thanks for the coffee and for telling me your stories."

"Not many young folks interested in the old days anymore." He engulfs my hand with both of his.

As I walk through the rain to the ferry terminal, I think about the old days. Dan shared a romantic memory of good ol', hard-working days when life was real. In those days, workers hauled heavy equipment into the wilderness and felt good about it. They left rusty barrels of toxic chemicals beside streams and pleaded innocence. Heck, they didn't need to plead innocence, nobody noticed anyway. One thing about the good ol' days—at least they didn't have the technology to screw up the environment as fast as we do now.

Despite the homesteads, the fishing camps, the hovercraft and jet boats, I had felt the Stikine's wild heartbeat as I paddled. The salmon, the seals and the geese are the pulse of a living land. The human alterations are like a peeling coat of varnish. They'll flake away if we leave the watershed alone.

How much development is too much? Dams for sure. And roads. Access for trucks would attract loggers and more miners, eager to ship the land's natural wealth to southern markets. All-terrain vehicles would roam off the road, up into the fragile alpine tundra. Hunters and poachers would drive more nails into the coffin of wilderness. The Stikine's wild character would slip away.

When I'm 70 and lost in the past, some young whipper-snapper will ask about my time on the Stikine. I'll talk about the Grand Canyon. I'll talk about Dan and his riverboats. I'll talk about Tlingits and Tahltans.

I hope I won't have to talk about the ghost of the Stikine past and the final taming of the Great River.

Autumn mist beside the lower Stikine

(above) Juvenile pine siskins near the Stikine River delta

The Peel
Watershed

The Peel Watershed

"I hope I didn't drop any papers," said Juri Peepre, glancing at the clock distractedly. "We have 15 minutes. Stewart Elgie said we had to file this by five o'clock today or it could be disallowed." He laid the papers on the counter and checked them off against a master list. A secretary pressed a date stamp into an ink pad and stamped each paper with a flick of her wrist.

"There is a one hundred dollar registration fee," she said.

"Damn," said Juri. He looked at me. "Do you have any money?"

"I'll run down to the bank."

I pushed open the glass doors of the federal court and trotted down the stairs. I sprinted up Second Avenue, dodging pedestrians on the sidewalk and cars in the intersections. Fortunately there was no one in line at the TD bank machine. I shoved in my green card, punched in my number and grabbed the cash.

The door was locked when I returned to the court registry. I hammered on the glass. Juri saw me, hurried over and unlocked it. I gave him five twenties. "Well, I guess that's it," he said. "It's too late to back out now."

Juri had been soul-searching for the past couple of weeks, worrying whether the Canadian Parks and Wilderness Society (CPAWS) should sue the federal government over its mishandling of mining exploration on the Bonnet Plume River. Mining companies have played hardball for decades, lobbying and spending money to ensure unlimited, unregulated access to Yukon wildlands. Conservation groups have politely played by the rules—and lost consistently.

We walked back outside. A cool north wind blew up the Yukon River. Cumulus clouds played lazily over limestone outcrops on Grey Mountain. The world looked unchanged, even though we thought we'd taken a momentous step.

∕∕   ∙   ∕∕   ∙   ∕∕

If you look at a map of Canada, the Peel River's tributaries look like the fingers of an outstretched hand spread over the northeastern Yukon. Three rivers form the wild heart of the

(previous pages) Dall sheep lambs above the Snake River

Track of timber wolf beside the Peel River

Peel Watershed: the Wind, the Bonnet Plume and the Snake. These rivers parallel the border of the Northwest Territories, flowing north for more than 300 kilometres before mingling their waters with the Peel.

This is the Yukon's largest "unroaded" wilderness south of the Arctic Circle. The nearest road, the Dempster Highway linking Dawson City with Inuvik, is 200 kilometres to the west—as the raven flies. This country is wild, not like tamed, "managed" lands further south. How can anything be called wilderness if it no longer has its natural predator-prey relationships?

The Peel drainage supports healthy populations of Dall sheep, woodland caribou, moose, grizzly bears, wolverines and wolves. Golden eagles, gyrfalcons and peregrine falcons nest near the rivers. This land is an important part of the wintering ground of the famous Porcupine Caribou Herd.

Two northern First Nations have a long standing heritage of hunting, fishing, trapping and cultural development in the Peel watershed. Aboriginal cultural heritage is told by elders,

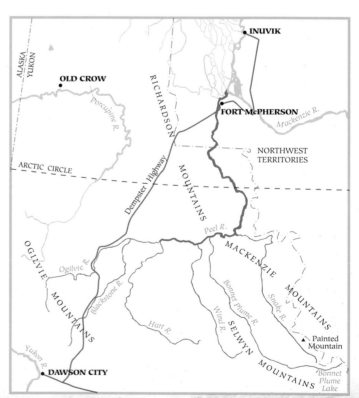

and can be found in ancient campsites, gravesites and the marks of stone adzes on tree trunks.

The Tet'lit Gwich'in have depended upon the Peel's unpolluted waters for thousands of years. The Gwich'in maintain their traditional activities to this day, travelling nearly 300 kilometres up the Peel River to the mouth of the Bonnet Plume and beyond. The Peel River flows past their fish camps and their main population centre in Fort McPherson, Northwest Territories.

The Nacho N'y'ak Dun First Nation of Mayo, Yukon also recognizes the importance of this region to its people. Their land claims final agreement calls for the Bonnet Plume to be nominated as a "heritage river." The Canadian Heritage Rivers System is a program to recognize Canada's important rivers and to manage them so their distinctive values are conserved. According to the background study, the Bonnet Plume overwhelmingly exceeds the Heritage River Board's selection criteria.

During the past few years, the main visitors to the Wind, Bonnet Plume and Snake rivers have been wilderness canoeists—and prospectors. Since neither the Yukon nor Canadian government had protected any wildlands in the watershed, conflict was inevitable.

Federal mining legislation in the Yukon reflects a romantic Klondike vision. Unfortunately, modern-day mining is no longer a lonely prospector with a pick and shovel. It is satellite imagery, helicopters and mammoth machinery. It is road building, blasting and unfathomably deep open-pits. It feeds on industrial growth and consumption, and can inflict enormous damage on the land. Its bottom line is money.

For close to a century, the Yukon has been the only place in Canada where miners can do exploratory work on mining claims without worrying about environmental regulations. At the moment, each claim is a kingdom with a mining company as its absolute ruler. Companies are free to clear trees, drill holes, scrape out road networks, build camps or trench entire hillsides. Concerned citizens have no recourse. Nor do the animals who lose their habitat. Proposed changes to the laws would leave the Yukon still hopelessly behind other Canadian jurisdictions.

Sunset and mountains beside the Bonnet Plume

In July, 1993, Westmin Resources applied to the Department of Indian Affairs and Northern Development (DIAND) for a permit to "walk" (a euphemism for the anything-but-gentle tread of heavy equipment) a pair of bulldozers to its claims beside the Bonnet Plume River. DIAND approved Westmin's application, describing potential environmental impacts in a mere five lines.

Westmin's heavy equipment roared across hundreds of kilometres of Yukon wildlands. Workers gouged out a mile long airstrip to allow for further access to their huge claim area. Just one of many blocks adjacent to the river contains more than five hundred connected stakings—a swath of claims 37 kilometres long.

The suit that Juri filed challenged the adequacy of the environmental screening. It asked why DIAND failed to consider that the Bonnet Plume had been nominated as a Canadian heritage river. Most importantly, the suit asked why DIAND ignored the potential impacts of the bulldozers once they reached Westmin's claims.

Postscript: It is December 1995, twenty months since Juri filed the suit. Today, he calls to tell me the bad news. His voice sounds as bleak as the -40° weather outside. He tells me that the judge noted that the Yukon Quartz Mining Act is based on an 1898 set of regulations. Despite this, Madame Justice Reed ruled that this Act supersedes any territorial land use regulations. The federal government has no authority to regulate environmental impacts on mining exploration. It will continue to be business as usual.

Stewart Elgie, a founder of the Canadian Sierra Legal Defence Fund and lead counsel for CPAWS says, "This ruling means that the 40,000 mineral claims in the Yukon are effectively an environmental law-free zone until the government enacts new legislation."

The judge did rap the federal government's knuckles for failing to take into account the Bonnet Plume's Heritage River nomination in its screening report. Unfortunately, it's too late. The bulldozers have already done their damage.

There must be a better way to decide the fate of wildlands.

HERITAGE RIVER BLUES

"It goes without saying," says the vice-president of Westmin Resources, "that we have the right to the quiet enjoyment of our mineral and property rights."

"Quiet enjoyment?" I interrupt, sitting up straight for a moment. "Does that mean you don't want noisy canoeists disturbing your D-9 drivers?"

"It's a legal term." He looks at me as if I'd crawled up out of a sewer to disturb his quiet enjoyment of the meeting of the Advisory Committee for the Bonnet Plume Heritage River Management Plan. Even the name of the committee is enough to put me to sleep.

I slouch back in my hard chair in the most imposing building in the downtown core of Mayo, Yukon. In Mayo, a town of a few hundred people, two storeys make a skyscraper. Downstairs is the liquor store and the post office. Next door is the library. The air in this conference room is stale. The conversation is bleak. The mining promoter explains how all-season roads, tailings, townsites, transmission lines and power production are compatible with wildlife habitat. Compatible with traditional lifestyles. Compatible with wilderness.

Soon it's my turn to expound the views of Friends of Yukon Rivers. "At the turn of the century, people in California thought there was unlimited wilderness in their state. Thirty years ago, that's what people in British Columbia thought. They were wrong. People who say that we have unlimited wilderness in the Yukon are just as wrong. No industrial development or roads should be allowed in the Bonnet Plume watershed."

"Excuse me," says the Westmin executive, "but roads don't destroy wilderness."

My mouth drops open. "Pardon me?" I'm not sure that I heard him correctly.

"Roads don't destroy wilderness," he says triumphantly. "People do!"

"Besides," says a member of the Mayo Chamber of Commerce, "what do rafters have to do with a local decision?"

A local decision? Mayo *is* the closest town to the Bonnet Plume, a fact which pleases the pro-development Yukon

Gwich'in children at a Peel River fish camp

government. What no one mentions is that the river is 160 kilometres away, over the rugged Selwyn Mountains, across the Arctic-Pacific divide. No one lives on the banks of the Bonnet Plume. A truly local decision would be a referendum of the caribou, sheep, grizzlies and marmots.

When these people go home and flush their toilets, the sewage flows into the Stewart River, towards the Pacific. Any mine pollution would flow away from Mayo, towards Fort McPherson, towards the Tet'lit Gwich'in.

I feel like an outsider, even though I've spent months travelling in the Peel River watershed. I even lived in Mayo for a year in the early '80s. An incident during my stay helps define my feelings about mines and roads along the Bonnet Plume.

The phone rang shortly after I arrived that September. "Are you the new teacher?" It was an old man who lived on the dirt road down by Danny's Department Store. "I hear you're interested in birds. Well, I have something for you. There's an extinct bird in my backyard!"

Who could resist that? I ran down the street and knocked on his door. "It's still here," he said. He hurried to his back window and pointed with a gnarled finger. "It seems incredible, but look! There, on the fence! A passenger pigeon!"

A bird book was propped open on his coffee table. The book must have been an antique, it still featured a painting of a passenger pigeon. They say that in the mid-1800s huge flocks of passenger pigeons darkened the sky like a solar eclipse. In one of the many shameful moments in our history, we clear-cut the deciduous forests that were the pigeons' home and slaughtered three billion of them within a few generations. In 1914, the last passenger pigeon died in the Cincinnati Zoo.

For a moment I fantasized that the bird on the back fence was a passenger pigeon, but I wasn't in a time warp, and extinction *is* forever. "It does look like the picture in this book. I wish you were right." I pointed to a similar bird on the next page. "This is what it is though, a mourning dove."

It has been more than a dozen years since I stared out the window at the mourning dove. Now I'm back in Mayo, and a placer miner is telling us what he thinks about extinction. "We can't get carried away about endangered species," he says earnestly. "We have to remember the human element."

As if we could forget.

"In any case," interjects a man standing against the wall, "what's the use of a pristine wilderness if it doesn't have a road so you can drive in to enjoy it?" I don't even try to argue with him. I'm surrounded by people who would agree with Wally Hickel, the ex-governor of Alaska, who said, "You just can't let nature run wild."

I'm afraid that this committee will ignore the biological genocide that humans are inflicting on the earth. I'm afraid the Yukon government has already decided how the report should read and we're a puppet committee to legitimize the process. I'm afraid the plan will be as short-sighted as the 1857 committee report on the game bill to the Ohio State Legislature:

"The Passenger Pigeon needs no protection. Wonderfully prolific, having the vast forests of the north as its breeding grounds, travelling hundreds of miles in search of food, it is here today, and elsewhere tomorrow, and no ordinary destruction can lessen them or be missed from the myriads that are yearly produced."

We are destroying wilderness as relentlessly as our great-great grandfathers destroyed passenger pigeons. I think back to my last trip through the Bonnet Plume watershed, another endangered wilderness....

*   *   *

It must be midnight, although the mountains are still bright with alpenglow. The sky is an inverted bowl, glazed bright to the north, fading to blues and eventually cobalt to the south. Here, just south of the Arctic Circle, dusk doesn't crawl down from a darkening sky. It crouches in the Bonnet Plume valley for a few hours until the morning sun chases it away again.

I'm baking cinnamon buns. The dutch oven is perched on a fire-pan beside the river. I toss a handful of driftwood twigs onto the bed of coals on the oven lid. A wisp of smoke curls upwards, then the dry wood ignites with a "whoosh."

I stand up, stretch and stare at the panorama of peaks through a pair of binoculars. "Is that blob below the snow patch a caribou or a rock?" I lower the binoculars and hand them to Kate Williams. I crouch down beside the cast-aluminum dutch oven and lift the lid. Almost done. The tops of the buns are deep brown, just starting to char. It's time for

Young marmot in the mountains between the Snake and Bonnet Plume rivers

some heat from underneath. I spread a few coals on the fire pan and plop the pot down.

"It's a rock," says Kate. "No. Wait a minute, it just moved. Maybe it's a grizzly."

We know grizzlies are in the area. The beach is crisscrossed with tracks, some distinct, some blurred by wind and rain. Caribou, wolf and grizzly tracks. Aldo Leopold, a father of the modern conservation movement, used the term "green fire" to describe those qualities that embody true wilderness: the howl of a wolf, a wolverine loping into the boreal forest...or grizzly tracks.

In the morning, we scatter the ashes and check to make sure we haven't forgotten a twist-tie or piece of aluminum foil. Most wilderness travellers are more meticulous about cleaning up around camp than they are in their own kitchens. We push the canoes into the river and paddle downstream.

It's a bright morning, the sunshine hot on the back of my neck. I swivel my visor around backwards. The river is swift but there are no rapids in sight. The rhythm of canoeing is like good music. I sink into it, paddling on auto-pilot and staring at the patterns of caribou lichen on a hillside, at a pair of northern shrikes in a spruce, at the cloud shadows on the alpine.

"Sideslip to the right," yells Richard Mueller from the bow of the canoe. I jam in a pry stroke while Richard draws. We slide sideways, but not fast enough. The canoe shudders as we grind over a granite boulder just under the surface. "We *almost* missed it," he says.

We're getting blasé after eight days on the river. We've left the Bonnet Plume's hardest whitewater upstream, but you have to pay attention on any moving water. This lapse only netted a gouge in the hull. It could have been worse. I straighten up and peer downstream.

Gradually, my eyes wander back to the mountains. I stare for a moment at a red-stained peak, then scan the slopes for Dall sheep, caribou or bears. I know we see only a tiny percentage of what is out there.

"Look at that," says Richard. I glance back at the river, expecting another rock or a set of waves. "There, in that stand of spruce trees."

Now I see it, and whatever it is, it's neon pink. We paddle forward and pull into an eddy. I grab the bow rope and slip a pair of half-hitches around a stubby willow. We clamber up the

bank, finding a mature spruce swathed in bright plastic flagging tape. With 180 shopping days left before Christmas, it can't be someone's warped idea of trimming and decorating their tree.

"It's a claim post," says Richard, pointing to a smaller tree that has been chopped, limbed, squared and attached to the spruce with ten metres of flagging.

I begin ripping down the excess tape. Surely a prospector can mark a claim without creating the riverside equivalent of Ogden Nash's billboard. I slide down the bank to the canoe carrying a football-sized wad of plastic. As we float northward we find another claim, and another. My collection of hot pink flagging grows and fills my day pack. Later we find out that these claims are the tip of the iceberg. Westmin Resources and other giant mining companies have staked a huge area adjacent to the Bonnet Plume.

It's tough to get much further away from civilization: 65° north latitude, tucked away near the Northwest Territories border. But even here, we can feel the hot breath of industrial development wafting up from the south.

The Bonnet Plume races out of the mountains to its confluence with the Peel. Because we lingered in the high country, hiking and enjoying the whitewater, we have to put in long days on the Peel. We're canoeing towards work schedules and deadlines.

It's our last morning on the river and my back is bent forward, my head leaning into an insistent headwind. I'm paddling hard but the canoe seems motionless, as if the Peel River's current plus our paddle strokes are perfectly balanced by the power of the wind.

Somewhere to the north there's a low pressure centre, a storm front marching across the islands of the high Arctic. Last night the storm hit us suddenly, turning our peaceful camp into something out of the movie *Typhoon*. In the grey half-light of midnight, the flying sand stung like a thousand tiny fire ants. The wind flattened a tent and a violent gust scooped up a canoe and cartwheeled it down the beach.

Today we're feeling just the edge of the storm's power— cold winds and rain slashing southwards up the Peel River. I dig my paddle into the water for another stroke and wonder when we'll see the ferry at Fort McPherson.

Rainbow in the Peel watershed

"Look," says Kate, "someone is waving from those cabins."

These are the first people we've seen since we paddled out of Bonnet Plume Lake—two weeks and nearly 600 kilometres upstream. We've floated past several fish camps along the Peel River in the last few days, but until now, no one has been at home. These camps are used by the Tet'lit Gwich'in people for netting and drying fish, hunting and teaching their children traditional activities.

Three little kids sprint down a dusty trail to the river. "Come up for a visit," yells the oldest boy, bouncing and pointing up the path. "Come have some tea."

Soon our four canoes are pulled up on the beach. I wonder if all eight of us should tramp up to the camp, but I don't need to worry about the hospitality of these people. Two women wait at the top of the bluff, mother and grandmother of our young guides. The older woman sits on the ground in front of a log cabin. She is nearly blind, but she's scraping a beaver skin with an ulu, a traditional knife. Her eyesight has faded, but her hands remember what to do.

"We're drying fish," yells one of the children. "Look in there, whitefish and conies."

A stack of burning willow branches smoulder in a fire pit on the dirt floor of the cabin. Pungent smoke eddies and swirls around rows of gutted fish hanging on racks suspended from the ceiling. The smoke seeps through the roof of the cabin and the smell of drying fish is heavy in the air.

"The coffee is just made," says the younger woman, "and the water is hot for tea."

We walk along a path to the white canvas tent that doubles as a kitchen. I accept a mug of tea gratefully and feel the warmth seep into my hands. The tea is thick and rich. I stir in a spoonful of sugar and a splash of canned milk.

"What do you think of the tea?" asks the woman. "It's mostly black tea, but we gathered Labrador tea leaves and mixed them in. Help yourself to some bannock or some biscuits."

I've felt close to the land during our trip down the Bonnet Plume and Peel rivers, but meeting three generations of Gwich'in at this fish camp makes me realize how transient a visitor I am. They've shown me another perspective of the land, a sense of permanence. Their land is largely unpolluted, largely unchanged after thousands of years of aboriginal use.

When we finish our tea and bannock, we'll paddle to Fort

McPherson. We'll pile our muddy gear into the back of a van and tie our canoes onto a trailer. We'll rattle down the Dempster Highway and stop at the Eagle Plains Lodge for supper and a beer. Tomorrow night I'll sleep in my own bed in Whitehorse.

These people will stay in the Peel watershed, living a tradition of thousands of years.

N   N   N

"Future mining development will not adversely affect the water quality or quantity of the Bonnet Plume," says the Westmin executive.

He doesn't mention that his company was charged in 1989 for the destruction of fish habitat in British Columbia's Strathcona Provincial Park. The company paid an $80,000 fine, after being convicted of allowing toxic acidic waste to leak from tailings ponds into a fish-bearing stream. I think back to Peel River fish hanging in a smoke house.

Another day, another Heritage River meeting.

I look across the table at Willard Hagen, president of the Tet'lit Gwich'in Tribal Council. Last night he told me, "The real gold in the Bonnet Plume is in the scenery." Then he was quiet for a moment, remembering what the country looked like. "If you find the other kind of gold, the mineral kind, maybe you should leave it in the ground."

During these Heritage River meetings, Willard Hagen, along with Chief Joe Charlie and an elder, Charlie Snowshoe, have told us why the Bonnet Plume and Peel rivers are critical to their way of life. They've pointed out that the Gwich'in live directly downstream of any potential mine. They've made it clear that they aren't interested in setting a dollar figure as a pay-off for any development that threatens the wildlife, fish and water on their traditional lands.

"Mining can actually improve the environment," says "Mr. Westmin."

The advisory board meeting is supposed to be a consensus building exercise. It is my job to listen to all opinions, to *hear* what they are saying. But I lose it.

"Come on!" I shout. "Are you telling me that you are going to improve the environment? Improve upon four billion years of evolution? Give me a break." I slump back down in my seat.

"Hold on," says the facilitator firmly, "let's not get excited. Mining *can* improve the natural world." The facilitator, chosen by the Yukon government, is supposed to be neutral. "There was once a pit down on Vancouver Island, an ugly gravel pit. But then they turned it into"—there was a pregnant pause while he prepared to pull a rabbit out of his hat— "Butchart Gardens!"

Silence hangs over the table like smog over Los Angeles. Even the miners seem a little embarrassed. Butchart Gardens? I think, what does a show garden have to do with large scale open-pit mining? I try, but I can't think of a come-back. Outside, a varied thrush whistles. I wish I was out there with it.

Fortunately, Willard Hagen is thinking more clearly than I. He leans over the table and says in a firm voice, a voice that carries the authority of his aboriginal heritage in the Peel River watershed. "Does this mean you are planning to plant pansies beside the Bonnet Plume?"

Dryas seed pods beside the Bonnet Plume River

(right) Fireweed above the Snake River

GRIZZLY THOUGHTS

Rain drums monotonously on the tent. I unzip the fly and peer outside. Streamers of fog slide down from the leaden sky and swirl between scattered spruce trees. Not far above camp it's snowing. The gigantic stripes of red and ochre rock on Painted Mountain glow behind a translucent layer of fresh snow. Mid-summer in the northern Yukon. I pull on long underwear, a wool sweater and a rain suit and dash for the shelter of the tarp.

"It's another Juri Peepre T-shirt day," booms Glen. "Thirty-eight degrees Fahrenheit, according to my thermometer." It's the fourth straight day of frigid drizzle since we flew into the headwaters of the Snake River. Glen won't let Juri forget that he told everyone to bring shorts, T-shirts and sunscreen. Juri also insisted that Glen limit his personal gear to one large dry-bag.

The object of this trip is to introduce some key people to the endangered wilderness in the Peel Watershed. In their real lives (unreal lives?), environmental activists breathe too much stale air. They hunch over too many computer screens, suffer through too many meetings, listen to too many boring bureaucrats. We're confident that the natural electricity of these wildlands will recharge everyone's batteries.

Along with Juri and I are Glen Davis, a generous donor and promoter of the World Wildlife Fund's Endangered Spaces Program, Stewart Elgie, founder of the Canadian Sierra Legal Defence Fund, Mary Granskou, executive director of the Canadian Parks and Wilderness Society, and Ron Cruikshank who works for the Tet'lit Gwich'in.

We had hoped to hike into the alpine, but gloomy clouds parked on the ridges are spitting rain at us. There is no point spending another day under the tarp, so we break camp and load the canoes. Stewart is my partner today. I soon discover that he is witty, articulate and intelligent—but surely he prepares legal briefs with more brilliance than he prepared for this trip. He packed a 1,200-page novel by Ayn Rand, a bottle of brandy, and a ten-pound bag of trail mix. He left behind warm clothes and decent rain gear.

Caribou killed by a grizzly

His footwear is particularly suspect. Today, he is trying the plastic bag trick: an inner layer of semi-dry socks, a plastic bag tied at the ankles and a second wet pair of socks squeezed into sodden running shoes. Stewart's main paddling goal is to keep the river where it belongs, out of our boat. He backpaddles furiously at the first hint of whitewater. Unfortunately, even small waves slosh into our heavily loaded canoe, pooling into frigid puddles at Stewart's feet.

We splash around a corner and see a young Dall ram standing on a clay bank. Downstream there are a dozen more sheep and five caribou. We back ferry to shore and pull up the canoes. Stewart limps down the beach, clumping on his numb feet like a skier in downhill boots.

"There must be a mineral lick here." I pull out my camera case and tripod. "There were sheep and caribou on that hillside last year as well."

Glen stares at Juri as he flips the latches on his camera case and lifts out a video camera. "Look at those lenses," says Glen. "They're bigger than an extra fleece jacket would have been. How much does that video camera weigh?" He looks at Stewart for a moment and then yells, "Stewart! Do you want to borrow a T-shirt? Juri made me bring an extra one."

We watch and photograph the wildlife, then push off downstream. While we paddle, Stewart tells me about life in the big city and our chances in the Bonnet Plume lawsuit. "Hey," he says, "I wonder why Juri and Glen pulled over?"

They are standing solemnly on a sand bar, looking down at a young caribou sprawled in a bloody heap. There's a football-sized hole in its shoulder. Its rib cage is torn open and entrails spill onto the beach. The rocks and gravel are stained with blood, like red chalk marks outlining a murder victim.

"There are grizzly tracks here," says Stewart as we nose our boat into an eddy and tie it to a snag.

"I've heard that grizzlies often bed down near a fresh kill," says Juri.

"It would be interesting to camp nearby and watch for the bear," says Glen. He calls grizzlies his "Icon Species." One of Glen's goals is to preserve living spaces for large predators, and by doing so, protect a tremendous number of other species as well.

The rest of us look from the caribou to the bush, wondering if eyes are watching us. I feel a prickling on the back of my neck. Tiny hairs stand on end, a physical memory of wildness dating back to primate ancestors. Many people think we've evolved above and beyond wild instincts. They are wrong. I'm exhilarated at knowing a grizzly is nearby. The bloody caribou is not a television image I can unplug or a book I can put down. In the Peel watershed, natural processes proceed at their own pace.

In most of North America, this is no longer so. Since Columbus stepped ashore five centuries ago, carnivore ranges have shrunk behind the relentless spread of Western culture. The traditional range of grizzlies extended down the west coast deep into Mexico and east to the Great Plains. The expanding frontier first collided with grizzlies in 1804, when Lewis and Clark slogged overland to the Pacific.

The expedition ascended the Missouri River, crossed the Rockies and travelled down the Columbia River to salt water. The high plains were thick with wildlife: bison, elk, deer, wolves and bears. Meriwether Clark described the grizzly as "a verry large and turrible looking animal, which we found verry hard to kill." Despite the "turrible" difficulty, Lewis and Clark did their "verry" utmost to rid the west of grizzlies. They shot and killed 43 bears, the first casualties in a largely one-sided war that continues to this day.

In California, all grizzlies were slaughtered by 1922. In Oregon, they were wiped out by 1931. In Arizona, 1935. A single old sow grizzly hid in the mountains of Colorado until 1979—when a bow-hunter killed it. I wonder if that archer strokes the bear rug with pride, gaining added pleasure from knowing it was the last one.

The few wildlands that grizzlies still roam in the northern U.S. are too small, too fragmented, too isolated. Movement corridors have been severed by highways and strip malls. DNA studies show that grizzly populations in the U.S. and southern Canada have diminished genetic diversity—they are becoming inbred. In B.C. and Alberta, grizzlies are "blue-listed" as a vulnerable species. They are threatened by habitat loss, hunting, poaching, killing of "problem bears" and road kills.

Evening light in the mountains above the Snake River

Even the Canadian Rocky Mountains national parks aren't a long-term refuge for grizzlies. A "parks are for people" development frenzy has exploded in Banff and Jasper. Ski resorts, golf courses, campgrounds, highways, hotels, restaurants, shopping malls and parking lots sprawl across critical habitat. Grizzlies are wilderness-dependent; they don't co-exist with roads and masses of people.

Some people actually prefer sanitized, pasteurized, grizzly-free national parks like Yosemite in California. To reach their favourite park they zoom along highways in fragile automobiles, passing accident scenes with smoking wrecks and the flashing lights of ambulances. They cheerfully put up with increasingly violent crime in crowded campgrounds— but the only grizzly they want is the nice, safe one waving on the state flag. Banff and Jasper may soon join Yosemite as others in a long line of de-clawed wilderness areas.

The six of us paddling the Snake River have chosen to visit the land of the grizzly. We are willing to risk the consequences of an "encounter," although that doesn't necessarily mean camping beside a bear's next meal. During my decades of wilderness travel, I've had just one brush with a feeding grizzly. I was paddling northwestern British Columbia's Nakina River with my friend Poco Bartels. It was a night I won't forget....

"You'll see grizzlies on the Nakina for sure," I said. "We saw five last time." Poco nodded skeptically. He had been looking for grizzlies unsuccessfully all summer. This river trip was his last chance before he drove home to California.

The Nakina flows into the Taku, an international river that empties into the Pacific just south of Juneau, Alaska. I had been along on the first descent of the Nakina two years earlier. We had encountered difficult rapids, deep canyons, rotting salmon—and sleek, well-fed grizzlies.

Poco and I paddled and portaged for five days, before the Nakina flushed us out of its canyon. Ragged-looking bald eagles launched from tree tops. They were moulting and their tails and wings had the jagged profile of a hockey player's teeth. Salmon darted under our kayaks. The rank smell of decaying fish rekindled visions of bears: muscular haunches,

glistening eyes, strong jaws. We could see bear tracks on sandy beaches, winding between salmon carcasses. Around each corner I expected to see a grizzly blocking the narrow stream.

"We've probably passed a dozen grizzlies already," said Poco. "I bet they're all hiding in the woods."

At dusk we stopped at a gently sloping gravel beach. We carried our camping gear to a clearing in the forest. Poco was a snorer. Sleeping near him was like bedding down under a volcano—you never knew when he'd erupt in sleep-shattering grunts and moans. Since he valued his friendships, he always brought his own tent.

It was Poco's turn to cook supper. While he lit the stove and rummaged in plastic bags, I walked to the river for a pot of water. Salmon chased each other in the shallows. The river gurgled and plopped with frenzied spawners. A dead salmon stared at me with glassy eyes, one bite nibbled from its gut. It smelled fishy. It smelled like bears.

We were tired and went to bed as soon as it got dark. I wriggled into my sleeping bag and chucked my clothes to the foot of the tent. I switched on my headlamp and opened a book. Something moved down by the river. Something big.

"Poco," I whispered, "did you hear that?"

"Yeah." Then he yelled, "Come ooooooon, sissy." Poco had bellowed this periodically during the summer—a joking machismo challenge for any grizzly that cared to listen.

It suddenly became eerily quiet. No snapping of twigs. No splashing of salmon. I imagined a bear, standing on its hind legs, trying to remove the salmon stench from its nostrils, trying to catch our scent. Then the grizzly snarled. "Poco," I said urgently, "have you got the bear spray?" Our can of bear repellent, a toxic blend of capsicum and oil designed to spray in the face of an attacking bear, was outside his tent.

"Yeah…but I can't get the fucking lid off."

I unzipped my sleeping bag. I pulled a sweater over my head, put on pants and boots and crawled into the night. From Poco's tent came a loud hiss. He swore and rolled out of his tent in an spicy, orange cloud. Poco had removed the lid, but not in the manufacturer's recommended way.

The Snake River

Something crashed through the undergrowth. Something with deep-throated rhythmic breathing. I ran to a stand of cottonwoods. The branches were dead, brittle, untrustworthy, but two of the trunks grew close together. I braced my back against one tree, pushed my feet against the other, and squirmed upwards, feeling grateful for my rock climbing experience. I found a branch strong enough to hold my weight. I hoped it was higher than a grizzly's reach.

"Poco," I shouted, "why don't you climb a tree?"

His back to a tree trunk, Poco stood like Clint Eastwood. The bear sprayer was his six-shooter. "I'd never get up one," he said calmly. "Besides, I'm covered in cayenne. I'm safe unless it's a grizzly with a taste for Mexican food."

I wondered if I should rejoin Poco on the ground in a display of solidarity. The grizzly roared. I stayed in the tree. I stood on my branch for a long time, until the rustling and cracking and deep-breathing faded.

"It's gone," said Poco. "Let's light a fire." My arms ached from clutching the tree, so I slid to the ground. I collected thin, dry twigs while Poco shredded cardboard from a box of pasta. Soon a crackling fire lit the ring of cottonwoods surrounding our clearing, but made the forest behind seem darker. The bear was nearby, somewhere in the darkness.

"My hands are burning," Poco said. "That spray is worse than jalepeño juice." I opened a water bottle and rinsed his hands. "Shit, I must have rubbed my eyes!" I grabbed another bottle and sluiced his eyes. The water cascaded over his face and dribbled onto his jacket. "It's getting worse." He ground his knuckles into his eyes. "Jesus, I can't see at all!"

"Maybe I should refill the water bottles," I said nervously, hoping he'd tell me not to bother. He didn't.

I picked up the bottles and the bear sprayer and tiptoed to the river. Every few steps I swung my headlamp in a semi-circle. No glowing eyes. I filled the bottles, jerking my head up each time a salmon jumped. I hurried to the fire, doused his eyes and pulled apart the first-aid kit looking for painkillers. I gave him a couple of capsules loaded with codeine and walked back to the river.

"I can see a little," said Poco after I'd made three harrowing trips for water. "It's blurry, but getting better."

"I'm going to bed," I told him.

"You'll never get to sleep," he warned.

I pulled up the stakes holding down my tent and dragged it closer to the fire. I crawled in. I left my clothes and boots on and pulled my sleeping bag around me like a shawl. The door was wide open. I lay awake, listening to Poco breaking twigs and feeding the fire. A throaty growl pulled me from the twilight world between consciousness and sleep. "It's back," yelled Poco.

I sprang from the tent, or tried to. The sleeping bag twisted around my legs like a boa constrictor and I toppled over in the dirt, struggling feebly. I kicked myself free, sprinted to the trees and climbed upwards. I waited until the rustling died out before returning to earth.

"This is ridiculous," said Poco. "I'm going to sleep." I tried too, listening to the normally soothing sounds of the river. Every splash was a heavy paw in the water. Every gurgle a wading grizzly. I gave up and returned to the fire. Another breaking branch propelled Poco from his tent and me up the tree.

The night stretched on, like an interminable B-movie. After a while we were too exhausted to care. We collapsed in our tents and slept fitfully until dawn. I felt awful, but Poco looked worse. The whites of his eyes were yellow and veined with blood. His face looked poached.

"I'm a wreck and I didn't even get to see the bear," he said. "I told you we wouldn't see any grizzlies on this trip."

⚡ ⚡ ⚡

We snap a few pictures of the dead caribou beside the Snake, then gravitate to the canoes. We stop to camp several hours later, below a hillside that is dotted with white blotches. Juri pulls out his spotting scope, mounts it on a tripod and counts Dall sheep. "I see 18," he says, "and there are bound to be more behind the ridge."

"I wonder if the bear is back at the caribou?" says Glen.

I'm wondering too, wishing I were a mosquito on the gravel bar upstream. Like Glen, I feel that grizzlies embody the essence of wildness. But even though I acknowledge a link with wild nature, I can't pretend that I'm a natural part of the Peel Watershed. We made the right decision to let the grizzly finish its meal without being harassed by a crowd of nosy humans.

"I've got good news and bad news," shouts Glen. "The good news is, it has stopped raining. Now it's snowing. Get those extra T-shirts out."

We carry a canoe up from the water and overturn it beside a patch of blossoming fireweed. Juri shakes out the tarp and ties it to the thwarts of the canoe. We stake out the sides, light the stove and brew tea. I reach into my dry bag and pull out a jacket and a wool hat.

The Dall sheep on the hillside and the grizzly feeding on the caribou upstream are oblivious to the weather. To them we must seem frail: pale animals that shiver and hide at the first hint of cold weather. They don't appreciate that we are technological creatures. They are unaware of our potential for needless violence, our self-righteous consumption of resources, our overpopulation, our restless urge to remake the world to suit our culture.

I hope they don't learn about us the hard way.

Dutch oven baking beside the Snake River

Grizzly bear (photograph by George Wuerthner)

The Skagway Watershed

The Skagway Watershed

On August 17, 1896, Skookum Jim, Tagish Charlie and George Carmack staked placer claims on Bonanza Creek. Their lucky strike was the spark that ignited the Klondike Gold Rush. Carmack later said, "I felt as if I had just dealt myself a royal flush in the game of life, and the whole world was a jackpot."

The news electrified the bush telegraph. Prospectors working in Alaska strapped picks and gold pans on their kits and headed for Dawson. The outside world heard about the Klondike a year after the original strike, when ships carrying tons of gold steamed into Seattle and San Francisco.

Newspaper headlines that blazoned "Klondike or Bust" fired the imagination of hundreds of thousands of people. Steamship companies sold berths with ads crying "Ho! For the Klondike." In a collective delirium, people from around the world headed north: a reporter from Chicago, the heavyweight boxing champion of the British Empire, a fruit farmer from Fresno—even Calamity Jane.

There were no easy routes to the Klondike. The best that can be said of the trails from Skagway, Alaska, is that they were less horrendous than the other options. In mid-summer, 1897, the first gold rush steamers disgorged their cargoes of people, horses, food and supplies on the beach at the mouth of the Skagway River. The stampeders felled trees, cleared brush and hacked out the town of Skagway, a settlement born of intemperance and anarchy.

By mid-winter in 1898, 5,000 people waited impatiently in Skagway. Sam Steele, a legendary figure from the North West Mounted Police, said Skagway "was about the roughest place on earth." A man caught stealing from a cache was lashed to a pole outside his tent, shot, and left hanging for three days as an example. Soapy Smith ruled the town with his outlaw gang until he too felt the bloody bullets of frontier justice.

Gold-crazed prospectors had the choice of two routes over the rugged Coast Mountains: the White Pass Trail or the Chilkoot Trail. The Chilkoot became a symbol of the

Klondike—a solid line of humanity trudging towards the summit, every back bent under a massive load of supplies. The White Pass was easier but longer. The stampeders' brutal treatment of horses became infamous, a shameful episode that haunted many White Pass veterans for the remainder of their lives.

Major J.M. Walsh crossed the White Pass to become the Commissioner of the Yukon. He described the scene: "Thousands of packhorses lie dead along the way…in tangled masses filling the mud-holes and furnishing the only footing for our poor pack animals on the march."

The twin lines of stampeders converged at Bennett Lake and floated down the Yukon River system to Dawson. More straggled into Dawson via the Stikine River trail, via the "all-Canadian route" through Edmonton, and via the "rich man's route" (by steamer up the Yukon River from St. Michael, Alaska). By July, 1898, Dawson's population of 30,000 made it Canada's largest city west of Winnipeg—the "San Francisco of the North."

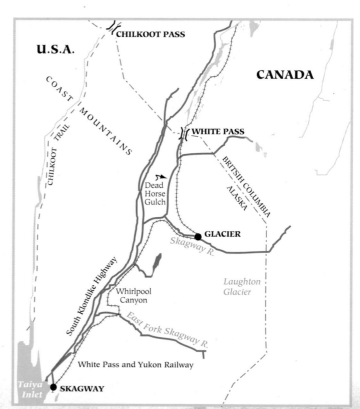

(previous pages) Jody loads his kayak into a White Pass train in Skagway

Bald eagle in a cottonwood tree

While the main mass of Klondike gold-seekers inched towards Dawson, investors decided to cash in on the stampede with an audacious plan—a narrow-gauge railway over the White Pass. The White Pass and Yukon Railway laid out the first tracks on Broadway Street in Skagway in May, 1898.

Workers blasted the roadbed out of solid rock. They tunnelled through a granite mountainside. They slogged through avalanches and bitterly cold winters. They built the highest railway bridge in the world at that time—a spectacular steel cantilever bridge 215 feet above Dead Horse Gulch. The first train chugged over the White Pass to the shores of Bennett Lake in July, 1899. A year later the line was extended to Whitehorse.

The story of the railway's proponents parallels the story of most Klondike stampeders—they didn't strike it rich. By the time the White Pass track was completed, the gold rush was over. Dawson's flame of life had burned white-hot for a single year while the easy pickings lasted. Then the fire burned low and Dawson gradually became little more than a ghost town. The railway limped along, barely solvent, carrying a few tourists and ore from mines in the Yukon interior.

The White Pass & Yukon Corporation shut down the railway in the early 1980s. In the 1990s, the trains again began chugging over the pass, cashing in on an increasing tourist trade. The railway survives on romance and history, serving the gargantuan cruise ships that dock in Skagway.

✗   ✗   ✗

Gold-fever is an addiction, an insane struggle for money and the power that it buys. People are still fascinated by visions of the Klondike: ill-prepared stampeders struggling against overwhelming odds, gambling their lives in a quest for the golden grail, accepting hardship with sheep-like resignation. Only a lust for gold could explain it. Only a fellow human could understand it.

Current tourist trade in Skagway and the Yukon is fixated on Klondike memorabilia. The natural history of the north

Mushrooms and ferns near the Skagway River

takes a distant second place. Thousands of years of aboriginal history is even farther removed from our modern imagination.

The Yukon licence plate has the logo of a squatting prospector swishing gravel in a gold pan. Many First Nations people object to celebrating the gold rush on the licence plate—to them, the coming of the stampeders was more a plague than a boon. A few years ago the Yukon's social-democratic NDP government decided to redesign the licence plate.

The outcry was incredible. Old-time Yukoners screamed in self-righteous anger. "Save the Goldpanner" bumper-stickers appeared all over the territory. Petitions swamped the legislative assembly. The government backed down, but it may have been the straw that broke their political back. In the next election, a gang of politicians who revere development came to power.

The Klondike evokes a romantic image of resource exploitation. To find the rich ground of the 1990s version of the Klondike, look on the floor of stock exchanges and around polished boardroom tables. Homespun wool clothes have given way to designer suits. You can amass golden nuggets without freezing your ass and blunting your fingernails in boulder-strewn creeks. You can build your fortune without ever seeing the impacts of your investments on the natural world.

Modern stampeders want to push back the frontier and unlock the remaining "wealth" in the Yukon. Wealth in this context does not mean the intrinsic wealth of intact ecosystems, wilderness and healthy wildlife populations. It means cutting down forests, digging open-pit mines and building roads and dams. Developers pretend that negative impacts won't occur in the north.

They are fooling themselves. Or trying to fool us. Natural disasters have already happened. One can be traced directly back to the construction of access routes between the coast and the Yukon interior.

Halfway between Skagway and Whitehorse is the community of Carcross. The name Carcross is shortened from two words—Caribou Crossing. Before the days of trains and automobiles, thousands of caribou crossed at the narrows between Bennett and Tagish lakes. The herd was decimated

by overhunting and loss of habitat made possible by road and railway. Nowadays, *Carcross* is definitely more appropriate than Caribou Crossing. There are more cars on the South Klondike Highway than caribou left in the remnant herd in the mountains.

People feel shame about episodes like the inhumane treatment of horses on the White Pass. But when wildlife dies as a result of industrial development or road-building, we're able to shrug it off, as if it has nothing to do with our actions. The fate of the Carcross Caribou Herd is not a romantic image. It is a real legacy of the Klondike.

A White Pass train rumbles above the Skagway River

(above) Hanging lichens in the forest

PADDLING DOWN THE WHITE PASS

It was Jody's idea. I had no interest. Canyons, dense rainforest, waterfalls: those were the only things I knew about the Skagway River.

"It'll be great," Jody insisted. "We can go light and do the river in one day." He was like water dripping against stone. He wore me down. I called the White Pass railway office in Skagway.

"Hello. What would it cost to ship a pair of kayaks up to Glacier?" There was a long silence. "Hello?"

"In the 20 years I've lived here, no one has paddled the Skagway River."

"I haven't heard of anyone either."

"The river is turbulent and dangerous. There are good reasons it has never been attempted before."

"That could be."

"Well." He sighed loudly. "We believe, here in Alaska, as you do in the Yukon, that you have the God-given right to kill yourself. But before we can take you to Glacier, we will require two things."

"What?"

"First, we will require you to sign a release absolving White Pass railway of any responsibility for your act. Second, we will require that you check in with the Chief of Police for the City of Skagway. If something goes wrong, God forbid, they will know that you are out there."

I put down the phone, feeling unsettled. I felt unprepared, like a city-slicker arriving in Skagway with patent leather shoes and a pair of suitcases, headed for the Klondike gold fields. Society's attitudes about danger and adventure have changed since 1898. Then, advertisers lured innocent people to the White Pass with exaggerations and downright lies. Now we can't even board a train without signing a liability release.

We arrive at the terminal near dawn. A porter hands us neatly typed papers saying that White Pass is not responsible for our foolishness. In duplicate. He leads us to the caboose and helps load our kayaks. Then he slaps me on the back.

"Good luck!" he says cheerfully. "The locals are taking bets on whether you'll survive."

The train chugs out of the station. Soon the broad valley becomes a ravine, squeezed between rugged mountains. "Ladies and gentlemen," squawks a loudspeaker, "if you look out the left side of the train, you'll see Whirlpool Canyon on the Skagway River."

I squash my nose against the window and peer down at a series of unrunnable cascades. The train rattles across a rickety-looking wooden trestle. The coastal forest looks impenetrable and screens any further glimpses of the river. We sit back until the train whistles to a stop near the Skagway River's glacial headwaters. We pull our kayaks out of the caboose, lay them on the tracks and watch the train lurch off towards Dead Horse Gulch.

We load our kayaks and launch into a steep rock garden below the railway bridge. I ricochet between boulders, do the limbo under an overhanging branch and shoot into an eddy. Jody isn't quite so lucky. His kayak swings broadside and the current's irresistible force pins him between a pair of boulders. He leans downstream and grabs a rock. I hop out of my kayak and throw him a rope. He ejects from his boat and pendulums to shore, clinging to the rope with one hand.

"My spare clothes are soaked," he says, upending his boat and draining out the water. We don't have much in our boats, just a bare minimum of emergency gear: one micro-thin sleeping bag between us, a couple of sweaters, a few chocolate bars. We're planning to sleep in our own beds tonight. It is only 20 kilometres to Skagway; surely we'll be off the river before dark.

We paddle cautiously, stopping to scout each time the river disappears around a corner with a flirtatious swirl of white. We portage occasionally, hauling our kayaks across the boulder-strewn shore. Late in the afternoon the river plunges into a canyon. It looks like a long portage. We clip slings onto our kayaks and drag them into the shadowy rainforest.

Lime-green lichen drips from spruce and hemlock branches. Mushrooms, from tiny yellow wafers to red spheres

Jody inspecting one of the Skagway River's unrunnable rapids

as large as a grapefruit, sprout from the spongy moss. Needle-sharp devil's club tears at my long underwear.

Time stands still as we inch through the primeval forest. The river is gone, its voice deadened by the greenery. Our horizons have dwindled to our kayaks, the tangle of deadfall and the next patch of devil's club. The forest looks untouched by humans. Maybe the Klondike stampeders stayed across the river, on the railway grade.

The forest looks pristine, but the watershed has changed from a century ago. The Klondike Highway is five kilometres downstream, on the opposite side of the river from the tracks. The valley is the filling in a "road and rail sandwich." It is unnaturally quiet, as if a giant Hoover has vacuumed away every large creature except Jody and I. No moose have crashed through the underbrush recently. No bears have chewed the juicy blueberries that dangle temptingly from bushes.

We drop our boats and gorge on berries. "I think I'll mosey down and see what the river is like." I grovel through the undergrowth, eventually emerging from the gloom at the top of a granite cliff. There are nasty rapids below me. Then the river vanishes. Literally. It's swallowed by the cavernous jaws of the earth. I've never seen anything like it.

"Can we start paddling yet?" asks Jody when I rejoin him.

"Sure, if you want to go on a journey to the centre of the earth. A landslide must have buried the river ages ago."

We drag our kayaks for another hour, then lower them down a gully below the river's exit from its underground tunnel. It's almost dusk and I'm tired. There will be no more paddling today. Jody's head disappears into his kayak, searching for food. I find a semi-level patch of moss under an overhanging granite shelf. We debate whether to use the spare clothing and sleeping bag as mattress or blankets. We shiver until dawn.

One sleepless night and I'm a wreck. The gold-seekers struggling over the Chilkoot or White Pass trails must have endured dozens of miserable nights. Maybe a regular diet of hardship toughens your body and spirit—either that or destroys them.

In the morning, we split a chocolate bar and squirm into our kayaks. Our last crumbs of food are gone by mid-morning.

By mid-afternoon we are still creeping along, paddling difficult rapids, portaging frequently. Rain begins to leak from the overcast skies. At least we're within striking distance of the highway, a few hundred metres above us.

"We're not going to make Skagway today," says Jody, looking up the steep hillside bristling with devil's club and broken by vertical granite cliffs. Someone heading for the Klondike wouldn't have given up so easily. In our defence though, there were no simple bailout options in 1898.

Two sweaty hours later we wrench our boats over the highway guard rail to a pullout overlooking the Skagway valley. I peel off my dry-suit and sit down on my kayak. A tour bus wheels in and parks beside a tourist signpost. A crowd wearing polyester pants and clear vinyl rain hats emerges and waves video cameras at the scenery. I walk over to the sign.

I look at a fuzzy photo of toiling men. Below the picture is a quote from Superintendent Michael J. Heney, the driving force behind the building of the White Pass railway, "Give me enough snoose and dynamite and I'll build you a road to Hell."

"Maybe that's what was missing," I mutter, "some snoose."

A blue-haired woman walks over to me and says, "You're not going down there, are you?" She grabs my biceps with a surprisingly strong grip, "My son kayaks back home in Vermont. I know the danger. You boys be careful."

A Winnebago turns off the highway. The driver, a young man wearing a cowboy hat and a bolo tie, stares in his rear-view mirror and backs up next to the sign. The woman in the passenger seat clutches the latest issue of *People Magazine*. With the motor idling, they read about the "Trail of '98" without soiling their shoes on the pavement.

They're younger than me. They can't be older than 35. Jody and I may not be as tough as the stampeders of a century ago, but it could be worse.

Spring breakup

(above) Berry bouquet near the Skagway River

The Yukon
Wildlands Project

The Yukon Wildlands Project

A WOLF

Once there was a wolf that lived in Montana's Flathead Valley. A biologist shot it with a sleep-inducing drug and fitted a radio-collar around its shaggy neck. When it awoke, ill and groggy, it tried to shake off the collar, but couldn't. Having no other choice, the wolf eventually accepted the collar, not knowing or caring that someone in a laboratory was following its movements.

One day the wolf trotted north. It wasn't lost. How can a creature supremely adapted to the natural world become lost? For some reason it didn't return to the Flathead, but loped into Canada, ignoring the international border, as it should.

No human can imagine the wolf's feelings as it approached its first major road, the Crowsnest Highway. We know that large carnivores like grizzlies and wolves avoid roads when they can. In the Southern Rockies, road kill is the leading cause of death for wolves. Maybe the highway was quiet. Maybe the wolf skipped across the geometrically straight slash of lifeless pavement with no feeling of danger.

In Banff, the wolf may have felt the earthquake rumble of Canadian Pacific Railway cars before it saw the tracks. No romance here for a wolf, no songs in its head about steel rails linking the country. It slipped across quickly, snorting to rid finely-tuned nostrils of the overpowering stench of chemically-treated railway ties.

The Trans-Canada Highway was a tougher barrier, a continuous stream of rolling cars and eighteen-wheelers. Hypnotized by the deadly glare of headlights, the wolf played Russian roulette. It scampered over the divided highway, screaming metal beasts attacking from one direction, then the other. It escaped into the healing forest, where the sound of the wind through a billion needles drowned the traffic noise.

It continued moving, through Jasper, across the Canadian National Railway, across the Yellowhead Highway, towards

(previous pages) Clearing of a storm at Lowell Lake, a widening of the Alsek River at the terminus of the Lowell Glacier

Boreal owl nesting in a dead tree

a new land and a chance to fulfil the biological urge that drove it north. A chance to mate, to rear pups, and in so doing keep the wolf population genetically strong. Unknowingly, the wolf was being swept along in the river of evolution that has flowed over the earth for four billion years.

The wolf had travelled more than a thousand kilometres when it became entangled in the web of roads near Dawson Creek, B.C. The now familiar roar of an automobile engine signalled its destiny—not a mate, but the bullet from a high-powered rifle.

A DREAM

The wolf story is based on the life of a real animal. The wolf's travels have clear implications for those of us who care about wildlands:

• Large carnivores need huge ranges.
• Wild creatures must be free to move to keep populations genetically healthy.
• Humankind, with its mastery over technology (or is it the other way around?), threatens the other species on our planet.

Large carnivores—wolves, grizzlies, wolverines, mountain lions, jaguars, sea turtles—can be viewed as "umbrella species," the wild earth's equivalent of a canary in a coal mine. If large carnivores are indeed appropriate indicators of the health of our ecosystems, then most of North America is in critical condition.

A decade or so ago, biologists began making global links between crashing plant and animal populations. Species from frogs to orchids to songbirds were on a critical downward spiral. Researchers concluded that we are living in the middle of the earth's sixth great extinction. The last one, the disappearance of the dinosaurs, took place 65 million years ago. Past extinction spasms occurred over spans of 10,000 to 100,000 years. What is terrifying about the current extinction pattern is the rate of loss. Some scientists have estimated that 15 per cent of all species could vanish within the next decade.

Most of our parks do not adequately protect plant and

animal species. Traditionally they have been selected for their scenery and recreation potential—only recently has biological richness become a factor. The vast majority of our protected areas are too small, and have become isolated islands in a sea of development.

For more than a century, conservationists have been fighting soul-numbing battles against destructive projects. Every time we manage to knock one down, a dozen others spring up in its place. We need an entirely new vision. We need to dream of what a biologically healthy North America would look like. We need to dream about a continent where our descendants live in balance with wolverines, bison, warblers, marmots and bears. We need to dream… then wake up and make it happen.

Since 1989, conservation groups across Canada have supported the World Wildlife Fund's Endangered Spaces Campaign. The campaign generated unprecedented public support for protecting representative samples of every natural region across the country. The mission of a new initiative, called the Wildlands Project, is to protect and restore the ecological richness and native biodiversity throughout North America through a vast system of connected protected areas. In every region of the continent, grassroots organizations are now working on Wildlands Project goals.

The concept is simple. We must set aside large core areas that exclude roads, machines, industrial development and agriculture. Buffer zones will permit human activities that do not threaten the life processes within core protected areas. The final step is to link reserves with biological corridors that allow for seasonal migrations, for re-population should local extinctions occur and for genetic exchange as animals move between different regions.

The concept is simple, but achieving it may not be. Much of the continent will need to undergo a healing process before native species will be able to return. We will need to deal with our own overpopulation and overconsumption. Many North Americans act as though happiness is dependent upon a 4,000-square-foot house, a motor home, three cars, a television in every bedroom and a cottage by the lake. We must re-learn to find joy within simpler lifestyles.

Full moon above the upper Stikine River

Many of us, scientists and conservation activists alike, feel that the human species is at a crossroads. We can accelerate down the development and consumption highway, expecting the gods of technology to find magical solutions to the crises we create. We can raze the forests, pave the grasslands, pollute the oceans. We can ride our planet through the heavens like a cowboy on a bronco, kicking our spurs into the living earth, trailing a cloud of extinct species behind us like a comet's tail.

Or we can slow down and savour the natural beauty of our world. We can live in harmony with the plants and animals that have evolved along with us. We can protect large wilderness areas that are the planet's treasure house of evolution.

A NORTHERN DREAM

Many people still dream of the Yukon as an "untouched" wilderness. The dream may become a nightmare. You don't have to look far to see the fingerprints of development all over northern ecosystems. So far though, the north has escaped the tide of extinction that is sweeping across the world. The Yukon has been given the gift of time, time to learn from the mistakes that have been made elsewhere.

Unfortunately, the clock is ticking swiftly:

• Two generations ago there were no roads in the Yukon. Now more than 10,000 kilometres of roads and other vehicle access routes form a spaghetti pattern across the territory.

• The Carcross Caribou Herd has been decimated by overhunting and loss of habitat made possible by roads and railways.

• Large-scale mining development threatens the Peel River watershed, the Yukon's largest wilderness south of the Arctic Circle.

• The Yukon's antiquated mining laws currently allow companies to stake and explore with little or no environmental assessment. Changes are proposed—but new legislation is unlikely to satisfy environmental concerns.

• Loggers are clear-cutting the old-growth boreal forests in southeast Yukon at an alarming pace.

• The Yukon government continued its controversial wolf

109

kill in the Aishihik region. During the 1995 season, the government switched from helicopter shooting to snaring. Wolves dangled alive in snares for up to three days before being found and shot. Moose, coyotes and wolverines were "incidentally" snared.

• The calving ground of the Porcupine Caribou Herd is still under siege from multinational oil companies. The Gwich'in from the Yukon and Alaska have been fighting oil exploration and development in the Arctic National Wildlife Refuge for decades.

Environmental organizations in the Yukon have created the Yukon Wildlands Project. We are determined to work with First Nations, governments, citizen groups—anyone with an honest desire to protect not just remnants of the natural world, but complete functioning ecosystems. It is a big dream—but the land demands no less.

The Yukon Wildlands Project is the northern anchor of the "Yellowstone to Yukon" Biodiversity Strategy. It is an audacious plan, one that gathers together scientists and environmentalists working on both sides of the international border. The strategy is to work towards a comprehensive protected area network that will ensure the survival of wildlands in the northern Rocky Mountains.

THE SPIRIT OF THE GREAT BEAR

Sow grizzlies no longer nurse cubs in the foothills of the southern Rockies. Grizzlies no longer scoop salmon from the shores of the Klamath River. The bears are gone, but their spirit remains—they are called ghost bears. Grizzly images are found on statues, in paintings, on flags and etched in stone petroglyphs. They are also indelibly etched in our imaginations.

The Wildlands dream is an inclusive one, one that allows for healthy lifestyles for humans—and makes room for wild things. In the Yukon, we are determined that living grizzlies do not become ghost bears. If grizzlies are forced to make a last stand in the north, many of us will be on their side of the battle lines.

If we act with wisdom, wild populations will remain strong and genetically healthy. As lands further south gradually heal from the wounds inflicted by our technological culture, grizzlies and other wild species will be able to re-inhabit their traditional range. Grizzly foot prints may once again be found beside streams in the Great Plains and the Sierra Nevada.

Bull moose during the rutting season

(above) The Bonnet Plume River

How you can help

The Yukon is a huge land, with a population of only 30,000 people. Most of the money that drives resource extraction and development in the north comes from investors in southern Canada and the United States. The Yukon Wildlands Project needs a strong southern constituency to support its work and give it a good chance at success.

Canadian Parks and Wilderness Society (CPAWS)-Yukon
30 Dawson Road
Whitehorse, Yukon, Canada Y1A 3L8
phone and fax: (403) 668-6321
e-mail: peepre@web.net

Yukon Conservation Society
Box 4163
Whitehorse, Yukon, Canada Y1A 3T3
phone: (403) 668-5678, fax: (403) 668-6637
e-mail: nornet@web.apc.org

Friends of Yukon Rivers
21 Klondike Road
Whitehorse, Yukon, Canada Y1A 3L8
phone: (403) 668-7370

Please find out which organizations in your region are working on Wildlands Project goals. For the plan to work, people who know and love the land in each region of the continent must work together. For information about local involvement, please contact one of these cooperating organizations.

Canadian Parks and Wilderness Society
401 Richmond Street West, Suite 380
Toronto, Ontario, Canada M5V 3A8
phone: (416) 979-2720, fax: (416) 979-3155
e-mail: cpaws@web.net

World Wildlife Fund
90 Eglinton Avenue East, Suite 504
Toronto, Ontario, Canada M4P 2Z7
phone: (416) 489-8800, fax: (416) 489-3611

The Wildlands Project
Box 5365
Tucson, Arizona, USA 85703
phone: (520) 884-0875, fax: (520) 884-0962

credit: Wendy Boothroyd

About the author

Ken Madsen is an award-winning writer, photographer and adventurer, living in Whitehorse, Yukon. He is the author of two other books, *Paddling in the Yukon* and *Tatshenshini Wilderness Quest*. His articles and photographs have appeared in numerous books and magazines including *Canadian Geographic*, *Explore*, *Paddler*, *Beautiful B.C.*, *Canoe*, *Up Here*, *Tatshenshini—River Wild* and *Protecting Canada's Endangered Spaces: An Owner's Manual*.

Ken works to protect North America's fast disappearing wilderness heritage. He was instrumental in the campaign that resulted in the establishment of the Tatshenshini-Alsek Wilderness Park. He helped to establish the Yukon Wildlands Project and is currently president of Friends of Yukon Rivers.

Ken is known in canoeing and kayaking circles for his exploits, including the first Canadian descent of notorious Turnback Canyon and the first complete descent of the Stikine River in northern British Columbia. He has paddled in many places around the world and has organized many "first descents" in the north.

About Lost Moose

Lost Moose, the Yukon Publishers—books from the North about the North. Write, fax or e-mail us for a current catalogue and price list.

Lost Moose Publishing
58 Kluane Crescent
Whitehorse, Yukon
Canada Y1A 3G7
phone (403) 668-5076, 668-3441
fax (403) 668-6223
e-mail: lmoose@yknet.yk.ca
web site: http://www.yukonweb.com/business/lost_moose

Also from Lost Moose
Alsek's ABC Adventure

Chilkoot Trail, Heritage Route to the Klondike

Law of the Yukon, A Pictorial History of the Mounted Police in the Yukon

Whitehorse & Area Hikes & Bikes

Yukon—Colour of the Land

Skookum's North, The "PAWS" Collection

Edge of the River, Heart of the City

Klondike Ho!

Another Lost Whole Moose Catalogue

The ORIGINAL Lost Whole Moose Catalogue

THE YUKON PUBLISHERS